How to Start a Restaurant on a Budget

By J. H. Dies

A Newbiz Playbook Publication

FIRST EDITION
ISBN – 13: 978-1546939894

For downloadable tools emailed directly to you please email **products@newbizplaybook.com** use the password Restauranteur in the re: of the email

For my family, the answer to my why

Chapter 1

Understanding Your "Product"

The fundamental truth about a great restaurant is that the product is, for those who join you, an experience. A fantastic experience will be spoiled by disappointing food. The reverse is also true.

Successful restaurants treat every customer as if they were a guest in their own homes. I have always favored restaurants referring to customers as guests, because the word carries a level of closeness that many restaurants never achieve. Having employees and leadership use this as part of their everyday language, can be transformative in making this experience a reality.

It is worth breaking down this element into its parts for more detailed discussion.

Lead with experience as opposed to food, because all too often the new restaurant owner only cares about food. Food is quite obviously critical, but in making decisions about budgets, timing and the space where the restaurant will be located, experience is an afterthought.

Is your place a cozy hangout for friends to have comfort food at a slightly rowdy noise level with a locally brewed beer, or are you looking to create a more elite dining experience in a quiet dimly lit romantic environment? Is there a rowdy German Band entertaining the crowd, or will you require a large storage system for a diverse offering of the finest wines? If this is your first experience starting a restaurant, we will encourage even the most accomplished chef's to begin with a casual style dining experience. This will be helpful for keeping costs at a minimum, and expanding the client pool with a more frequent dining fit.

New restauranteurs tend to think of food and menus simply in terms of taste, and offering a widely attractive menu that favors the individual talents and recipes of new business owners. This, in my opinion, coupled with poor decisions about buildout and equipment expenditures are among the reasons most restaurants fail when they do.

This book will provide ideas, not only for testing your concept, or starting with a lower economic commitment, but also for setting up your business to succeed with food planning. Food, for example, should be seen as a hard expense. Good flavor, consistency, and food quality must be a given to succeed, and we will cover ideas on how to ensure success here. From the beginning, a smart restaurant owner will create a menu that limits the different foods required, while maximizing dish flexibility with sauces, preparation labor, seasoning, and preparation styles. Food shelf life is also a factor, so that in the beginning extensive amounts of food are not wasted or lost. Frankly, beverages tend to be the most profitable items in most restaurants, and often have much more controllable shelf lives. They should absolutely be a part of planning.

Ignore these fundamental truths, and none of these contents will matter. Embrace them, and you will succeed. The goal is to create Raving Fans at every opportunity. The clients you help will have friends and family getting married, and you want them to insist on you to handle them.

Starting With a Plan

Many Restaurateurs start their businesses as caterers from home with a dream to one day open multiple locations, or even franchise a brand.

The business is a difficult one, and you should start with an idea of where you want to finish.

If you simply want to augment income, and have a talent for cooking, with no desire for anything more than a small locally based business, your journey is easier, but from the beginning, you need to think about your brand.

You should have a very detailed vision of the brand including experience and food. This should be in the form of a wish list with two parts. First, what are the must haves for consistent protection of the brand and image? Second, what would you like to add over time to cement or finalize the brand.

Many restauranteurs, especially first timers, focus on a business plan and getting funding from traditional lenders. This focus can be misplaced. Frankly, traditional financing is very difficult for first time restauranteurs without substantial private funding contribution. Don't worry. We will walk through that issue in this book, but for now we want to reduce risk. The business plan should have some empirical information about what works, or doesn't. Your approach may change, once you try some of the experiments we recommend, and in any case you will have empirical data that helps you and lenders know more about your chances of success.

Creating the Brand

Your brand to be effective must accomplish all of the following:

- It makes your business easily recognizable. The easier your business is to recognize, the more people will associate your business with a certain product or service. This in turn translates into more sales.

- It must be pleasing, fun, and a positive reflection on your offering. If you are all organic, or locally sourced, your brand should reflect what makes you better.

- The brand should be professional, and consistent with your product. Some brands do well with characters, or funny animation, a gourmet brand offering more expensive or exclusive fair, should be more serious. This is critical to avoiding customer confusion

- Your brand should be highly visible, from the restaurant signage or otherwise, and unique to you, so that customers can see it and instantly recognize what you offer.

- Your brand is much more than a logo, or catchy slogan, it is a feel you are trying to share with the customer that draws them to your business. Logo is important, but all of your branded items, should be consistent with each other, and contribute to a greater understanding of your business and offerings.

- All of the best brands are easy to remember and simple in design. The very best brands are the ones that you don't need to explain. Once a person sees the brand, he or she will immediately know what your business is all about.

- The best brands also hold an emotional appeal to the target market. The emotional connection that you will make will depend on the demographic, regional differences and psychographic profile of the target market. In other words, you have to know what makes them "tick". You have to know what strikes their emotional strings and work your brand identity on that.

- Lastly, your brand identity should be consistent. If you have multiple locations, they should be similarly decked out with signage a consistent feel.

Concept Testing

The high cost of starting a new restaurant under normal circumstances is very well known. Even fast food franchises are requiring mid six figure initial investments or more. The good news is that it is still very possible to test an initial concept, and even open doors to generate critical revenue without the full commitment required to begin a going concern.

This section will focus on three options for this testing that are well understood, and with which a number of budding startups have found true inspiration. Specifically, we will cover food trucks, popups, and private catering.

Restaurant Food Trucks

Food trucks have become a restaurant startup phenomenon. Cities have welcomed the variety of food, and the social environment that many food trucks in a local setting can create.

I have a book on food truck startups, called How to Start a Food Truck that goes into more detail but for purposes of this section there are a number of benefits of this approach:

1. Allows you to test a menu and restaurant concept without brick and mortar costs. You can even rent the truck!

2. Flexibility to travel to customers

3. Social media advertising for food truck can build brand loyalty before you ever open

We have included a food truck operation tool to provide an example of operational cost considerations.

Unless the plan is to start a fully functioning food truck business before attempting the brick and mortar restaurant, it will likely make sense to rent a truck if possible.

Food trucks can be very expensive to buy and/or design new. Don't unwittingly buy someone else's problem and tank a business with a poorly maintained used truck that will have constant repair problems.

Food Truck Operations Spreadsheet

Item	Monthly Estimated Cost	Notes
Parking or Host Charges	varies	You may have to pay for a stall, or pay a business a percentage of revenue to offer products to their employees
Phone / Internet	$100 - $200	
Fuel	$500	This will vary a lot.
Labor	8-15 dollars per hour	$8 - $15 per hour is average rate.
Repairs	$1,000	Just for protection
Food / Beverage Restock	varies based upon sales expect to replenish food stocks weekly, obviously if you have a great weekend, it may happen more often	
Paper Product Restock	$800-$1600	Depends on food cost and frequency of operation.
Insurance	$50 - $150	Depends on food cost and frequency of operation.
Total:		

Pop-Up Restaurants

One of the newest food trends is pop up restaurants. These can take a number of forms from posting a mobile cooking station in a parking lot with inexpensive signs, to rental of warehouses and open spaces, to temporary leasing of recently closed restaurants.

This can be a great way to raise funds for your actual restaurant, test a potential location (though don't assume that the short term interest in your restaurant will be sustained on its own).

Permit rules may vary depending on location. In some cases, the permit is tied to your business (which can share your brand's name), and may be used at more than one location. In other instances your permit may be temporary for the two weekends that you are open for example.

Catering

Many restauranteurs, got their start with catering before opening their own restaurant right away. Catering parties offers you the chance to plan menus, interact with customers, and take advantage of venues rented or provided by customers. Catering events such as weddings may require specialty expertise, but this allows for testing of food costs and other aspects of the restaurant business that may help avoid future road bumps.

This is an important approach to see if you are a good fit for the business, prior to spending massive time and money on something you might not enjoy.

We have included a number of tools applicable to catering, which could be helpful in pursuing this startup approach.

Immediately following this section is an example catering proposal and contract with some guidance on how to professionally test your approach by hosting an event as a caterer.

Electronic versions of the proposal and contract will be forwarded to any of our readers who request them through products@newbizplaybook.com. Put Restaurant Startup in the re section of the email.

How to Charge For Catering Services

A Huge Mistake New Caterers often make is failing to price their services for ALL costs.

You have overhead, costs of servers, time spent shopping for, preparing, delivering, and serving the food. We will provide a pricing tool herein, but you should have a detailed breakout of all of your hard costs for internal purposes, and a presentation of key breakdown of your retail pricing for the client.

We have illustrated this with the Catering Proposal Template tool below:

Catering Proposal Template

Prepared for:
[Client.FirstName] [Client.LastName]
[Client.Company]
Prepared by:
[Sender.FirstName] [Sender.LastName]
[Sender.Client]

{Include thumbnail photos of your delicious food, branding information etc. If you have candid photos of people enjoying your food at a well decorated event those are nice as we

[Date Today]

Dear [Client.FirstName] [Client.LastName]:

[Sender.Company] is pleased to provide you with the attached catering proposal for your [Event Occasion], which is currently scheduled to be held on [Event Date] at [Event Location]. We understand that this is a very important occasion and we are committed to giving our utmost attention to make this a very memorable and stress free day.

In addition to an assortment of the finest foods and beverages, a knowledgeable and experienced staff, [Sender.Company] boasts a wide selection of china and silverware. Furthermore, we have strong relationships with the area's best vendors for any additional needs. Your dedicated event planner will work with you to design the best possible event which will reflect your own personal tastes and preferences. We are confident we can deliver all of these services while staying within your desired catering budget.

The attached proposal represents [Sender.Company]'s formal offer to provide catering services for the event described therein, upon the terms and conditions and pricing provided. As planning begins, some of the details in this document will change to suit your preferences and priorities. Consider this proposal an initial overview of our offerings in conjunction to your needs, and should you have any questions about the possibilities, please do not hesitate to contact me directly at [Sender.Email] or [Sender.Phone].

Thank you for the opportunity to provide you with this catering proposal. We very much look forward to the opportunity to work with you and to make this occasion a momentous one.

Sincerely,

ABOUT US

[Sender.Company] has been in business for [Number] years. We fulfill distinct event needs with excitement and creativity, the finest quality ingredients, and flawless elegance.

You name the celebration, describe the look and feel you are going for, and then relax. And relax some more. [Sender.Company] takes care of every detail of your memorable event.

With our unparalleled service, you can count on us to provide you with everything you need for your big event. When you hire [Sender.Company] you are guaranteed one of the best events you will ever attend.

GENERAL INFORMATION AND PARAMETERS

- Attendance – [Number of Guests] people
  (client Initials) _____
- Event Date – [Event Date]
  (client Initials) _____
- Event Location – [Event Location]
  (client Initials) _____
- Event Description – [Event Occasion]
  (client Initials) _____
- Budget – [Budget]
  (client Initials) _____

EQUIPMENT RENTALS

Equipment Needed	Price	QTY	Subtotal
Tent	$500	1	$500

This is optional. In case of inclement weather, you may want to have your guests sheltered.

Dance floor	$10	10	$100

Price is per square foot, quantity reflects the number of square feet needed.

Sound equipment	$500	1	$500

If you plan to have any kind of emcee, the sound equipment would be necessary.

Linens	$800	1	$800

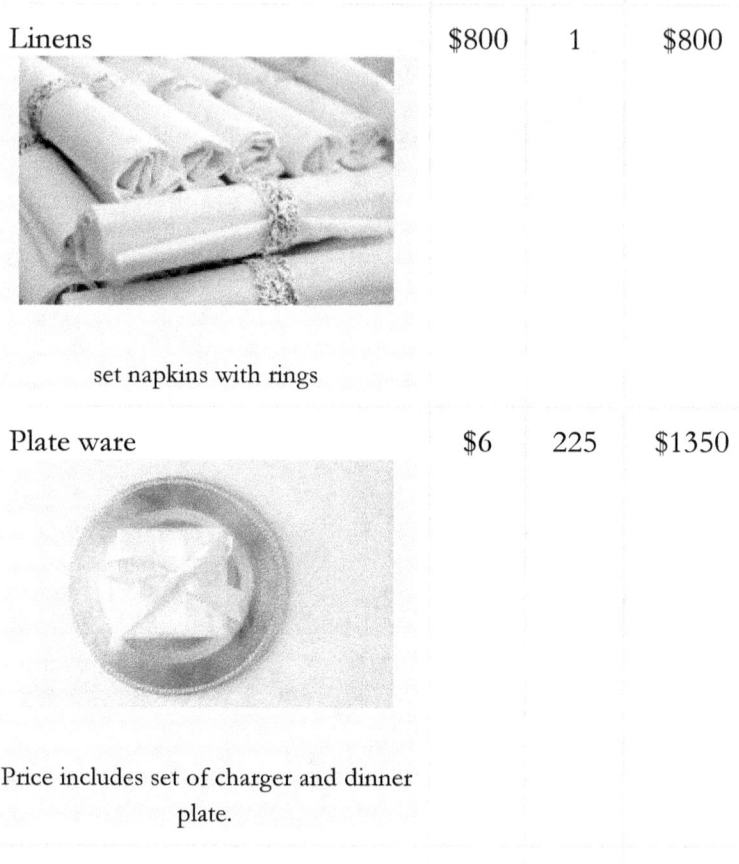

set napkins with rings

Plate ware	$6	225	$1350

Price includes set of charger and dinner plate.

Flatware	$4	225	$900

Price includes standard 5 piece setting.

Stemware $5   225 $1125

Price includes a water glass and wine
glass.

Tables and chairs $200   20 $4000

Due to your guest count, your event
needs about 20 tables. This could
change.

Total: $9275

(client Initials)   _____

MENU AND FOOD

1.   Appetizers – [Cost of Appetizers] per person
2.   Dinner – [Cost of Dinner Entree] per person
3.   Dessert – [Cost of Dessert] per person
4.   Drinks – [Cost of Drinks] per person

(client Initials) _____

EVENT STAFF

We pride ourselves with providing you with the absolute best service. This includes ensuring the best staff will be on hand to make your event absolutely incredible. You can sit back and relax and let our professional servers, bartenders, and chefs take care of all the work.

Staff Member	No. of Staff Needed	Cost per Staff Member
Servers	[Number Servers to Guests]	[Cost per Server]

Bartenders	[Number Bartenders to Guests]	[Cost per Bartender]
Chefs	[Number Chefs to Guests]	[Cost per Chef]
Event Manager	[Number Mgrs to Guests]	[Cost per Event Manager]
Event Planner	[Number Planners to Guests]	[Cost per Event Planner]
Rental Equipment Delivery	2	Included

A designated event planner from [Event Planning Company] will also be provided and will serve as the main point of contact for [Client.Company].

(client Initials) _____

DECORATIONS

Centerpieces – pricing in accordance with [Event Planning Company] catalog available online at [Event Planning Website Address]

Flowers – pricing in accordance with [Event Planning Company] catalog available online at [Event Planning Website Address]

Lighting – pricing in accordance with [Event Lighting Company] catalog available online at [Event Lighting Website address]

Tables and Chairs – pricing in accordance with [Catering Company] catalog available online at [Catering Company Website Address]

(client Initials) _____

ENTERTAINMENT

-       Band or DJ – from company
that [Client.Company] chooses. Contract will be separate
from any agreement with [Sender.Company]. Please let us
know if we can assist in helping you find the perfect
entertainment.

(client Initials) _____

PRICING AND TERMS

Name of Service	Price
Food for Cocktail Hour and Reception	$13000
Table and Chair Rental	$5000
Plateware, Flatware, and Stemware	$2500

Subtotal: $20500
Sales tax (3%): $615
Total: $21115

A **50% deposit** will be due on or before **[Deposit Due Date]**. The **remaining balance** will be collected **a week prior** to the event. We accept all major credit cards and checks.

The estimated amount above is **not a fixed** amount and is **subject to change** based on actual charges and final guest counts and **any additional charges** approved by the Client.

_____   _____

Signature Client   Date

Catering Equipment Contract Template

CATERING AGREEMENT

This is a catering agreement {"Agreement"} executed this {date} day of {month}, {year},

BETWEEN

Client
{Address}
{Other Contact Info},
Referred to hereafter in this Agreement as "Client,"

AND

Your Business Name
{Address}
{Other Contact Info},
Referred to hereafter in this Agreement as "Caterer."

Client and Caterer agree to the following:

1. Services

1.1 Caterer agrees to provide food services to the Client for {basic description of event}, known as the "Event," taking place on {date}.

1.2 For this Event, Caterer agrees to provide the following: {detailed description}

1.3 Client agrees to provide the following: {is the client providing equipment, venue, chairs etc}

2. Deposit

2.1 Client is required to pay a deposit of _____ upon signing this Agreement. (1/3 to 50% is normal here)

2.2 This deposit is not refundable, as it will be used to acquire food and equipment from third parties which cannot be returned.

3. Payment

3.1 For the above services, Client will pay Caterer a total of {amount of money, This can be a set price for a certain menu, assuming a certain number of guests, or it can be a price per guest attending the event, or any other arrangement you agree to. Be specific, so that there are no hidden costs} , including the deposit outlined in Section 1.

3.2 If the Client should request additional food or services that will add to the total cost agreed upon by this contract, such must be agreed to in writing, either as an addendum to this Agreement, or in a separate document.

3.3. The balance on the total cost for the Event is due   {at the end of Event, once all property has been returned to Client and/or Caterer, within 15 days of the Event, etc.}.

4. Guests

4.1 Client agrees to provide Caterer with the total number of guests no later than {number} days before Event.

4.2 Client agrees to break down the guest list into adults and children, and include any food allergies or special dietary requests, if applicable.

5. Menu

5.1 Client will {provide his/her own menu, choose from Caterer's available options, etc.}.

5.2 Menu must be confirmed by {length of time before the Event}, or else Client will be subjected to   {penalty fee amount}.

5.3 Menu will be fixed, and no changes may be made, {72 hours before Event, 24 hours before, etc.}.

6. Cancellation Policy

6.1 Client may cancel this Agreement {times when Client may cancel}.

6.2 Cancellation occurring {length of time} before Event will result in {a total forfeiture of deposit, loss of 50% of deposit, etc.}, as outlined in Section 2.

7. Arbitration

7.1 Should either party failure to provide or breach this Agreement in any way, the offending party will be liable for any damages.

7.2 Both parties agree to seek a third-party mediator or arbitrator for any disputes that arise as a result of this Agreement.

8. Jurisdiction

This Agreement falls under the jurisdiction of the state of {State}, and is therefore subject to all of {State's} laws and regulations.

Signed:

_____   _____
Client Name   Client Signature

_____   _____
Caterer Name   Caterer Signature

Date :_____

Starting a Small Restaurant

Finally, no matter how grandiose the vision, consider testing it by starting with a small restaurant.

Many new restaurateurs sabotage their business by overspending on high end equipment, exotic locations with long term leases, interior designers, and ridiculously priced signage.

For example, a number of successful restauranteurs have bootstrapped with neglected inexpensive, but well located spaces (that ironically may create a clever urban appeal).

Consider planning your equipment needs around your menu offering, with a plan to expand equipment as your concept gains traction. This may mean fewer menu options, but overdoing a menu at the start is a recipe for disaster. It impacts food cost, training and preparation, as well as the risk of clouding the brand or restaurant's theme.

New equipment is also not the best way to start your business. Frankly, restaurant auctions and local used equipment outlets and social media sales sites can get you equipment at pennies on the dollar. Another approach to consider is leasing equipment with a location (though for reasons we will discuss, taking over a prior failed location has its downside).

Even those whose model is intended to evolve into a more fine dining experience, this approach can be very successful. Great food, service and presentation will get customers buzzing no matter how humble the surroundings.

Tune out traditional restaurant advice. Put together your own budget and then ruthlessly try to chop it down so that everything you are buying is a "must-have" in your eatery on opening day. "

Think makeover. Look for a 1500-2000-square foot space in a rebounding area. It is fine to knock down office walls at the back of a former shop to make room for your kitchen, but be mindful of access to plumbing, electricity, and restrooms. These are not inexpensive upgrades.

Rent should be cheap. Aim for something in the neighborhood of $1,000 a month. Don't be afraid to be rejected. It may mean negotiating on a number of places at the same time, but there will be a landlord who is tired of losing money every month on an unrented space. Consider a short term lease clause that allows for an agreed increase in rent after six months, with a new long term lease. This gets you a chance to get in and succeed, and gives the landlord a chance to get a more fair rent if the restaurant hits its stride. At six months, a restaurant should be moving to a place of predictable revenues. Also consider negotiating length of the lease, exit or quitting clauses, and transferability of the lease.

Outdated fixtures and furnishings can be inexpensively removed and replaced with low-cost alternatives that fit your theme and look. Think super inexpensive tile, and creative decorative touches. Consider asking friends and family for help on this instead of asking for money. Many will be happy to help in this regard even if they are not comfortable investing actual cash in a first time restauranteur.

If the space is not built out for your purpose, consider asking the landlord to assist with a build out allowance, or a rent reduction for the first six months to make the economics viable. All of this is negotiable. Some restauranteurs are surprised to know that their landlords own equipment seized for rents or abandoned by other tenants from a different location.

Consider hiring local artists for murals, or to assist with creative signs. Negotiate signage allowances with the landlord. It is important that customers be able to find the location, but unchecked, signage can be damaging to the viability of your restaurant. Consider adapting a sign already in the space to fit your brand.

Equipment such as soda dispensers, can be worked around by renting the equipment, or event starting with bottled sodas, and inexpensive tea and water dispensers.

Finally consider barter. Many trades are willing to offer discounted prices for services or labor in exchange for feeding their crews etc. Take advantage of your strengths in keeping costs down.

There is a such thing as an inexpensive restaurant startup, and every dime you save, means a few more days you are open to give guests a chance to find you, and fall in love with your restaurant.

Chapter 2

Equipment Considerations for Your Catering Business

Transportation (for restaurants that will start with or offer catering or delivery):

> For most events a 15 passenger van with a row or two removed is a readily available, **rentable** vehicle that can be used to get large amounts of food to your venue efficiently. If you are using large heating cabinets, or have more food involved a box truck such as those available from U-Haul will do the trick.

> As your business grows, you may want a more custom vehicle with built in food warmers or refrigeration, but that should be down the road. Make sure rental costs or operation costs if you own are factored into your pricing.

> If you are going to offer delivery, consider using services like uber eats or others that subcontract such services. If you hire drivers, include in their hourly compensation a stipend for gas and wear and tear on vehicles. It is common to have a standard delivery charge for deliveries in your area, so this need not be a hard expense for your business.

Kitchen Equipment:

Common equipment needed for a kitchen will include: (Keep in mind you don't have to buy all of this at once!)

- Range
- Oven
- Grill
- Deep-fryer with baskets
- Several Refrigerators or Walk-in cooler
- Freezer (either a chest, or walk-in)
- Cold Storage Containers
- Dry Storage Containers
- Sauté pans
- Stock/soup pots (2 20quart and 2 40quart)
- Sauce pans
- Stainless pans for fry station, sauté station, and salad station
- Stainless box grater
- Vegetable peelers
- lemon/tomato wedge cutter
- Commercial food processor
- Table mount can opener
- Baking sheets
- Baking pans
- Hand Sink – Sanitizer and Signs
- Prep Table
- Tongs multiple sets
- Wooden spoons
- Spatulas
- Ladles
- Chef's knives
- Paper Towel Dispenser
- Whisks
- Mixing bowls

- Thermometers
- Steam table
- Entrée plates
- Inexpensive flatware
- Salt Pepper Shakers
- Bread Baskets
- Sugar/Sweetener Racks
- Pasta bowls
- Appetizer plates
- Salad plates
- Dessert Plates
- Tea / Water dispensers
- Refill Pitchers for full service
- Cleaning Rags
- Ice Bucket (specifically labeled for Ice Only)
- Cleaning buckets (specifically labled for cleaning products)
- Rubber floor mats
- Hand soap/ sanitizer dispenser
- High Chairs
- Fire extinguisher

If Bar Service is Offered

- Multi-fold Towel Dispenser
- Multi-fold Towels
- Soap Dispenser
- Anti- Bacterial Soap
- lemon boards
- paring knives
- drink mixer
- cocktail shakers
- mixing glasses
- cocktail strainers
- s/s ice scoops

- jumbo can punch
- bottle cap lifters
- set salt & pepper
- wine opener
- muddler
- zester
- condiment caddies
- Set drink mix containers (margarita, bloody Mary, sweet & sour etc.) with back up gallons, pints, quarts
- 10 inch stainless bar spoons
- glass rimmer
- ash trays
- bar mats
- tip trays
- Straws
- Beverage Napkins
- Sword Pics
- Low-Suds Glass Cleaner
- Rinse Sink Sanitizer
- Wine glasses
- carafes
- beer glasses
- glass chiller
- pitchers
- rocks glasses
- Collins glasses
- Martini glasses
- Irish coffee glasses

Cleaning supplies

- Squeegee
- Mop Buckets with Wringer and Mops
- Push and short handle brooms with dustpan
- Coffee decanter brush
- Cleaning solution bottles
- Wet floor signs
- 32 gallon grey trash can w/lids
- Rectangular trash cans

Chairs and Tables

Depending on your theme and brand, inexpensive tables can often be made, or built with readily available materials. A local German Pub has tables made from pallets that are solid on top, and were sanded and heavily stained. They are a great fit for the place.

One place not to skimp is chairs. Heavy patrons will break plastic chairs, embarrassing the guest, and exposing you to safety problems. Look hard for heavy duty inexpensive chairs.

Where to Buy Equipment

In the beginning, we recommend that caterers look for quality used equipment in good shape that can be found at auctions, on craigslist, and on eBay and other websites. The value and savings are substantial, and many very established caterers will only buy used equipment. Many large cities have used or discount restaurant supply companies. Spend the time to do your research here. This is a big place to save money.

Chapter 3

Restaurant Site Evaluation

Much is made of the importance of location to the viability of your restaurant. Once a decision is made as to the rough proximity of the proposed restaurant, multiple listing agents should be contacted to show various locations.

Don't just stick with one, as the competition amongst several can be used to your advantage in getting a great deal. Place higher emphasis on agents with experience in restaurants, and have them walk you through locations asking questions about how they envision the space being used.

It is rarely a good idea for a brand new restaurant concept to build a location on its own land. The costs can be overwhelming, and can cause these startups to fail. It is not uncommon to see a restaurant fail to open its doors at all because of poor planning on new construction and/or buildout.

A great way to plan for needs of your restaurant and buildout is to look at what franchises similar to your concept require of their new franchisees. Darden, for example (current owner of Olive Garden, Cheddar's, and others) publishes its site selection and layout criteria online. (see www.darden.com)

To assist with the aspects of evaluating a restaurant site, we have provided the following restaurant site checklist.

Restaurant Site Checklist

This checklist is to be used for evaluating potential spaces for viability as a restaurant location

Location

_____ Was this previously a restaurant (or restaurants?)

_____ If so, why did the prior restaurants fail? (Keep in mind that the local community may assume your restaurant is not worth going to if multiple prior restaurants didn't make it there. This is especially true if there were cleanliness/health code problems)

_____ Traffic – specifically is this located near other restaurants, movie theatres, anchor stores or shopping outlets etc? - Consider doing a traffic count during your planned operating hours – it will help for financing

_____ Timing of traffic – specifically is this a business lunch only type location, or can you serve brunch lunch and dinner here?

_____ Quality/Stability of the Neighborhood

_____ How much signage can be placed outside of meeting room, in common areas?

_____ Property Tax expenses if not born by landlord

_____ Proximity to other similar restaurants

Capacity

_____ Kitchen should be between 15-25% of the total space in your restaurant. If smaller you limit how much you can serve during a shift. If larger you are wasting space that could be used for customer seating.

_____ Reception Area (you need a place for guests waiting on tables to interact with a host on full service restaurants)

_____ Meeting Room

_____ Dining Area

_____ ADA disabled access to entire facility and bathrooms?

Bathrooms

_____ Will you need to provide extra amenities to make the room nicer
_____ Cleanliness – poorly kept restrooms reflect poorly managed venue
_____ Number of stalls vs. number of guests

Parking

_____ Existent (many restaurants lose business for poor parking)?
_____ Fee to use parking lot?
_____ Valets – included? Is there a preferred valet company?

_____ Buses – if using buses - is there room to turn around, unload?

_____ Is there preferred parking for certain tenants or other limitations that will block access to your guests

Entrance

_____ Opportunity to brand/decorate entrance area?

_____ Curb appeal; are you comfortable with the current look/feel of the entrance?

Electronic versions of this tool with room for notes are available upon request at **products@newbizplaybook.com**.

Chapter 4

Marketing for Restauranteurs

Of all the challenges a new restaurant owner faces, marketing the business can feel the most overwhelming. The good news is that you can very easily, and inexpensively market your business to a receptive target audience. The challenge will be follow-through and consistency in maintaining exposure for your brand.

Whole books have been written on the subject of marketing, and this material is not designed to replace them. Our hope is to provide you with guidance as to how to spend your time, and where. You should understand the pros and cons of the various options out there, to make intelligent decisions on your ROI or return on investment. Everyone has different results with different media. As important as this is to your success, you should track where your leads (especially the ones that generate revenue for you), are coming from. Advertising that appears expensive at the outset, maybe cheap relative to other options when you see the revenue it is generating.

Website/SEO

Your website if properly done can be a very useful marketing tool, and may be one of the places you spend early money, once you start getting gigs. Wordpress.org, has some incredibly easy templated websites that can get you started. If you can get to a place where you are on the first or second page of google with your site, which is very doable, this will be the single most effective marketing vehicle you have. Keep in mind, you aren't looking to be first when someone types restaurant." You are looking to be first when someone types "English Pub Cleveland." The difference between these two is what makes it vastly easier to rise to the top. I have, with no training whatsoever, been able to get several service based websites on the first page of google.

The key is to duplicate the search you want to be relevant for. For example, if the hope is that you come up first when someone types "great barbeque in St. Louis," do that search, and then go to the sites on the first page and a half of google, and look at the content. You are specifically looking for whether there are videos or pictures, how often your key search term appears in their script etcetera.

You are also looking for the titles used for the website's pages. For example if you click on a page, at the top right side of that page there will be a tab, with some language on it that is designed to summarize the content of that page. These are title tags, and this research on content, will tell you what you need to emulate to get to the top of google. Be careful. Copying text and directly duplicating material, or over using a few key words will get you punted from key word searches, which would kill the effectiveness of your website. When you start to grow your business, you should consider early investment in a great website with an SEO (search engine optimization) professional to help you.

We recommend that at a minimum, a third of all profits go back into the business to grow it and help with important investments in the business. This investment would be at the top of that list. If you have some resources already saved, this would boost visibility substantially and increase the speed with which your business gets noticed. There are a number of free-lance website development options out there. Do your research as this is a hugely important investment.

Sample Selling

Consider the local area, and businesses that might be in the market for your services, and take them samples! Many restaurants supplement their business by bringing boxed lunches, or catering once or twice per month to local businesses. Be sure to leave lunch menus in case executives want to order out. Even if the business doesn't hire you, if the people there love your food, they may share your name or business cards with others who will hire you. This is a great, practical, and inexpensive way to get noticed. Try to feed the office managers who often make food purchasing decisions for the company.

Networking and Word of Mouth

Experienced, successful restaurants will tell you that most of their new business comes from referrals and word of mouth.

The challenge is to reach the level where the "machine" is sending you leads on a constant basis. As you build relationships with guests, be sure to pay special attention in the form of offering a free drink or taste testing a new appetizer with customers who frequent your restaurant. Make them look important in front of their invited guests, and these folks will come back again and again. Encourage staff to pay attention, and let you know when repeat guests are in.

It is reasonable to demand promptness, professionalism, responsiveness, and elite service from your employees. Let them know that in your mind they are an extension of your brand, and if they provide an exceptional experience for your guests, it will mean more income for them, and for the restaurant.

Consider a free lunch card bowl for drawings. It will provide great data on who is going to your restaurant and where they work. These are common in restaurants for a reason.

In the beginning you should be very vocal to your personal network of friends and family to let them know you have begun to do this work, being sure to emphasize all of your efforts, research, and time spent getting to know the business.

Open Houses

In advance of holidays, and peak catering times, open your house, or shop to guests, and have them come in and taste your best. Offer a menu that would complement holiday parties befitting the time of year, perhaps with a feature cocktail, and use the time they are tasting your wears to meet potential clients, and get their feedback on your food.

Social Media

Social media is an incredibly effective and inexpensive means of advertising your business, and to a limited degree it is worth your time to learn how to get your brand up and running on Facebook, Instagram, twitter, Pinterest, and snapchat. This is how you build a following, and stay relevant to others who need to think of you first when they or someone they know decides to plan an event that requires catering. In the beginning these are free if not very inexpensive. Videos are more engaging than photos, which are more engaging than text. Offer different discounts in each media to test where your customers are coming from. Keep in mind with social media consistent updates are the name of the game. As your restaurant grows, this is another place where hiring a professional may make sense.

Ratings and specialty sites

There are a number of sites like Yelp, which allow businesses to put up very basic profiles for free. In the beginning, it can be helpful to put your site and business on as many of these as possible so that these sites point back to your website and business. When you sign up, you will be pitched on pay packages that help boost your chances of appearing early on these sites. In our experience these types of investment don't generate nearly as many live leads as search engine optimization. It is important to monitor these sites, and to regularly search for your site so that you can see what reviews are out there both good and bad, which could impact your business.

That said, you should regularly search google for reviews of your business. Many people look to these sites to see what customers are saying about the food and the experience. Bad reviews can be a killer.

Phone books, mailers and other print advertising

We address these last, because frankly they are not very effective in generating revenue relative to the cost, at least in this business. At some point, you may be large enough to require a better add in a phone book, or need to have mail outs for clients to stay in front of them, but getting email addresses, and electronic communication is vastly more effective. We simply don't recommend spending startup dollars here.

You may have need for printed material in the form of business cards or trifolds, which can be handed out to guests who have you in to cater. These are necessary expenditures, and when they are printed it should be high quality work on good card or paper stock. This stuff represents your brand, which must be elite if you want to command larger fees with your engagements.

We have included a great example of a tri fold in word form, so you don't have to play with formatting or make one yourself. Simply cut and paste photos or logos and add content as you see fit. Below is a printed example with two sides of a suggested layout, with content references that will allow you adjust the tri-fold to fit your business.

Electronic versions of this tool with room for notes are available upon request at **products@newbizplaybook.com**.

To get started right away, just tap any placeholder text (such as this) and start typing to replace it with your own.

This would be a great place for a mission statement.

You can use this fresh, professional brochure just as it is or easily customize it.

On the next page, we've added a few tips (like this one) to help you get started. To replace any tip text with your own, just tap it and begin typing.

Company Name
Street Address
City, ST ZIP

Recipient
Street Address
City, ST ZIP Code

replace with
LOGO

Tel Telephone
Fax Fax

Website
Email

**Company
Name**

**Products and
Services**

replace with
LOGO

Trifold Back

Think a document that looks this good has to be difficult to format? Think again!

- To easily apply any text formatting you see in this document with just a tap, on the Home tab of the ribbon, check out Styles.

- Use styles to easily format your Word documents in no time. For example, this text uses the List Bullet style.

Find even more easy-to-use tools on the Insert tab, such as to add a hyperlink, insert a comment, or add automatic page numbering.

View and edit this document in Word on your computer, tablet, or phone. You can edit text, easily insert content such as pictures, shapes, and tables, and seamlessly save the document to the cloud from Word on your Windows, Mac, Android, or iOS device.

So what do you include in a brochure like this?

We know you could go on for hours about how great your business is. (And we don't blame you—you're amazing!)

But since you need to keep it short and sweet here, maybe try a summary of competitive benefits at left and a brief success story here in the middle.

The right side of this page is perfect for those glowing testimonials and a list of key products or services.

Don't be shy! Show them how fabulous you are.

"Your company is the greatest. I can't imagine anyone living without you."

—Very smart customer

"This style is named Quote but you can also use it to call attention to an important piece of info."

—Your friends in Word

What you offer:

- Product or service
- Product or service
- Product or service
- Product or service

Your most impressive clients:

- Big, important company
- Another really well-known company

Chapter 5

Food and Beverage Planning

One of the most important aspects of great catering is food and beverage planning. The best recipes in the world will not overcome the failure to bring or cook enough food. A party will suffer if the bar falls short. Similarly, clients will be angry if they feel they are charged for large amounts of wasted food or drinks. For this reason we have included a food and beverage planning tool, which should insure that you are in good shape on these matters.

Food and Drink Consumption Planning Tool

Appetizers

As you determine the appetizer quantity, consider what purpose the appetizers will serve. If you're serving appetizers before a main meal, you don't need as many as you do if the appetizers are the meal itself. Because appetizers are different from other food items, how much you need depends on several factors. Appetizers don't lend themselves to a quantity chart, per se, but let the following list guide you:

- For appetizers preceding a full meal, you should have at least four different types of appetizers and six to eight pieces (total) per person. For example, say you have 20 guests. In that case, you'd need at least 120 total appetizer pieces.

- For appetizers without a meal, you should have at least six different types of appetizers. You should also have 12 to 15 pieces (total) per person. For example, if you have 20 guests, you need at least 240 total appetizer pieces. This estimate is for a three-hour party. Longer parties require more appetizers.

- The more variety you have, the smaller portion size each type of appetizer will need to have. Therefore, you don't need to make as much of any one particular appetizer.

- When you serve appetizers to a crowd, always include bulk-type appetizers. Bulk-type foods are items that aren't individually made, such as dips or spreads. If you forgo the dips and spreads, you'll end up making hundreds of individual appetizer items, which may push you over the edge. To calculate bulk items, assume 1 ounce equals 1 piece.

- Always try to have extra items, such as black and green olives and nuts, for extra filler.

When appetizers precede the meal, you should serve dinner within an hour. If more than an hour will pass before the meal, then you need to increase the number of appetizers. Once again, always err on the side of having too much rather than too little.

Quantity planning for soups, sides, main courses, and desserts

The following tables can help you determine how much food you need for some typical soups, sides, main courses, and desserts. If the item you're serving isn't listed here, you can probably find an item in the same food group to guide you.

You may notice a bit of a discrepancy between the serving per person and the crowd servings. The per-person serving is based on a plated affair (where someone else has placed the food on the plates and the plates are served to the guests). In contrast, buffet-style affairs typically figure at a lower serving per person because buffets typically feature more side dish items than a plated meal does. Don't use the quantity tables as an exact science; use them to guide you and help you make decisions for your particular crowd. If you're serving a dish that you know everyone loves, then make more than the table suggests. If you have a dish that isn't as popular, you can get by with less.

Soups and Stews

Soup or Stew	Per Person	Crowd of 25	Crowd of 50
Served as a first course	1 cup	5 quarts	2-1/2 gallons
Served as an entree	1-1/2 to 2 cups	2 to 2-1/2 gallons	4 gallons

Main Courses

Entree	Per Person	Crowd of 25	Crowd of 50
Baby-back ribs, pork spareribs, beef short ribs	1 pound	25 pounds	50 pounds
Casserole	N/A	Two or three 9-x-13-inch casseroles	Four or five 9-x-13-inch casseroles
Chicken, turkey, or duck (boneless)	1/2 pound	13 pounds	25 pounds
Chicken or turkey (with bones)	3/4 to 1 pound	19 pounds	38 pounds
Chili, stew, stroganoff, and other chopped meats	5 to 6 ounces	8 pounds	15 pounds
Ground beef	1/2 pound	13 pounds	25 pounds
Maine lobster (about 2 lbs. each)	1	25	50

Oysters, clams, and mussels (medium to large)	6 to 10 pieces	100 to 160 pieces	200 to 260 pieces
Pasta	4 to 5 ounces	7 pounds	16 pounds
Pork	14 ounces	22 pounds	44 pounds
Roast (with bone)	14 to 16 ounces	22 to 25 pounds	47 to 50 pounds
Roast cuts (boneless)	1/2 pound	13 pounds	25 pounds
Shrimp (large: 16 to 20 per pound)	5 to 7 shrimp	7 pounds	14 pounds
Steak cuts (T-bone, porterhouse, rib-eye)	16 to 24 ounces	16 to 24 ounces per person	16 to 24 ounces per person
Turkey (whole)	1 pound	25 pounds	50 pounds

Side Dishes

Side Dish	Per Person	Crowd of 25	Crowd of 50
Asparagus, carrots, cauliflower, broccoli, green beans, corn kernels, peas, black-eyed peas, and so on	3 to 4 ounces	4 pounds	8 pounds
Corn on the cob (broken in halves when serving buffet-style)	1 ear	20 ears	45 ears
Pasta (cooked)	2 to 3	3-1/2	7

	ounces	pounds	pounds
Potatoes and yams	1 (medium)	6 pounds	12 pounds
Rice and grains (cooked)	1-1/2 ounces	2-1/2 pounds	5 pounds

Side Salads

Ingredient	*Per Person*	*Crowd of 25*	*Crowd of 50*
Croutons (medium size)	N/A	2 cups	4 cups
Dressing (served on the side)	N/A	4 cups	8 cups
Fruit salad	N/A	3 quarts	6 quarts
Lettuce (iceberg or romaine)	N/A	4 heads	8 heads
Lettuce (butter or red leaf)	N/A	6 heads	12 heads
Potato or macaroni salad	N/A	8 pounds	16 pounds
Shredded cabbage for coleslaw	N/A	6 to 8 cups (about 1 large head of cabbage)	12 to 16 cups (about 2 large heads of cabbage)
Vegetables (such as tomato and cucumber)	N/A	3 cups	6 cups

Breads

Bread	Per Person	Crowd of 25	Crowd of 50
Croissants or muffins	1-1/2 per person	3-1/2 dozen	7 dozen
Dinner rolls	1-1/2 per person	3-1/2 dozen	7 dozen
French or Italian bread	N/A	Two 18-inch loaves	Four 18-inch loaves

Desserts

Dessert	Per Person	Crowd of 25	Crowd of 50
Brownies or bars	1 to 2 per person	2-1/2 to 3 dozen	5-1/2 to 6 dozen
Cheesecake	2-inch wedge	Two 9-inch cheesecakes	Four 9-inch cheesecakes
Cobbler	1 cup	Two 9-x-9-x-2-inch pans	Four 9-x-9-x-2-inch pans
Cookies	2 to 3	3 to 4 dozen	6 to 8 dozen
Ice cream or sorbet	8 ounces	1 gallon	2 gallons
Layered cake or angel food cake	1 slice	Two 8-inch cakes	Four 8-inch cakes

Pie	3-inch wedge	Two or three 9-inch pies	Four or five 9-inch pies
Pudding, trifles, custards, and the like	1 cup	1 gallon	2 gallons
Sheet cake	2-x-2-inch piece	1/4 sheet cake	1/2 sheet cake

Alcohol and Beverage Planning

Concerning drinks, let the following list guide you:

Soft drinks: One to two 8-ounce servings per person per hour.

Punch: One to two 4-ounce servings per person per hour.

Tea: One to two 8-ounce servings per person per hour.

Coffee: One to two 4-ounce servings per person per hour.

Water: Always provide it. Two standard serving pitchers per table are usually enough.

Again, err on the side of having too much. If people are eating a lot and having fun, they tend to consume more liquid.

Alcohol Consumption and Pricing Projection Tool

There is always some subjectivity in alcohol planning. The assumption here is that 75% of the guests are drinking alcohol. This should be discussed, as a higher percentage of children in attendance, a group of heavier drinkers etc., could impact these assumptions.

As always we recommend adding 10% to all estimates. You will frustrate guests if there is insufficient alcohol, so make sure they are in agreement with your assumptions on numbers. They will know their guests better than anyone. The cost estimates assume average costs on beer, wine, and liquor. Premium beer, wine, and liquor would also mean increased costs. This also assumes equal consumption i.e. 25% each of beer, wine, and liquor. Beer drinkers tend to range closer to 40%, but these figures make scaling for your needs much easier.

The following, which was originally designed for our wedding books, should help plan for alcohol consumption and beverage stocking in a restaurant. Keep in mind that orders may have to be made weekly for liquor, beer, and wine, so adjust projections for weekly consumption. Monitoring sales early will give a sense of adjustments that need to be made over time. The challenge is to not overstock, while still meeting guest needs. If a certain beer or liquor is stacking up, cut it from your order, because these inventory costs hurt your bottom line. BD = beer drinker, WD = wine drinker, LD = liquor drinker

	Small Wedding (100 guests)	
	Amount	Cost
Beer	5 cases per 25 BD	75.00
Wine	20 bottles per 25 WD	160.00
Liquor	6 750 ml bottles per 25 LD	90.00

	Medium Wedding (200 guests)	
	Amount	Cost
Beer	9 cases per 50 BD	135.00
Wine	40 bottles per 50 WD	320.00
Liquor	12 750 ml bottles per 50 LD	180.00

	Large Wedding (100)	
	Amount	Cost
Beer	3 Kegs 100 BD	270.00
Wine	79 bottles per 100 WD	632.00
Liquor	24 750 ml bottles per 100 LD	360.00

Electronic versions of this spreadsheet are available upon request at **products@newbizplaybook.com**.

Food Costing

Food cost can vary depending upon the menu, style of restaurant, and distance of the restaurant from the fare (i.e. high end fresh seafood will be more expensive in Kansas).

Quick dining options should have lower food cost aiming in the low to mid 20% range (20% of the price charged for the item).

Higher end restaurants should target 30% but expect as much as 40% for purposes of projections.

A number of strategies can be used to manage these costs such as:

- Balance the menu – there is a reason steak is often paired with potatoes which are a much lower cost item. It balances the total cost of the plate within reason for both the restaurant and the guest.

- Sizing portions - controlling portion sizes is critical to food cost, and your cook's best friend should be a scale. Every prep chef should be expected to weigh or size nearly every portion, not just for cost but also for consistency.

- Watch waste – the best restaurants train on avoiding waste and use items like protein bones and shrimp shells for soup stock etc. Make this a part of the restaurant's culture and it will pay off.

- Order wisely – keep as much data as you can on food waste and surplus. Some of the greatest barbeque restaurants in the country feature an item until they run out of it that day – creating urgency and insuring no waste. As the restaurant ages, data will help predict more accurately what is needed in each weekly order.

- Seasonal food – consider the cost swings in out of season produce, and guide your menu to more available less expensive foods

- In house prep – chopping and prep of your food is something a grocer will often charge much more for than the cost of a prep cook.

- Consider joining purchasing groups – these associations of small restaurants order together to take advantage of quantity pricing.

We have attached a screen shot of our recipe costing template, which can help accurately price menu items and project costs below.

Recipe Costing Template

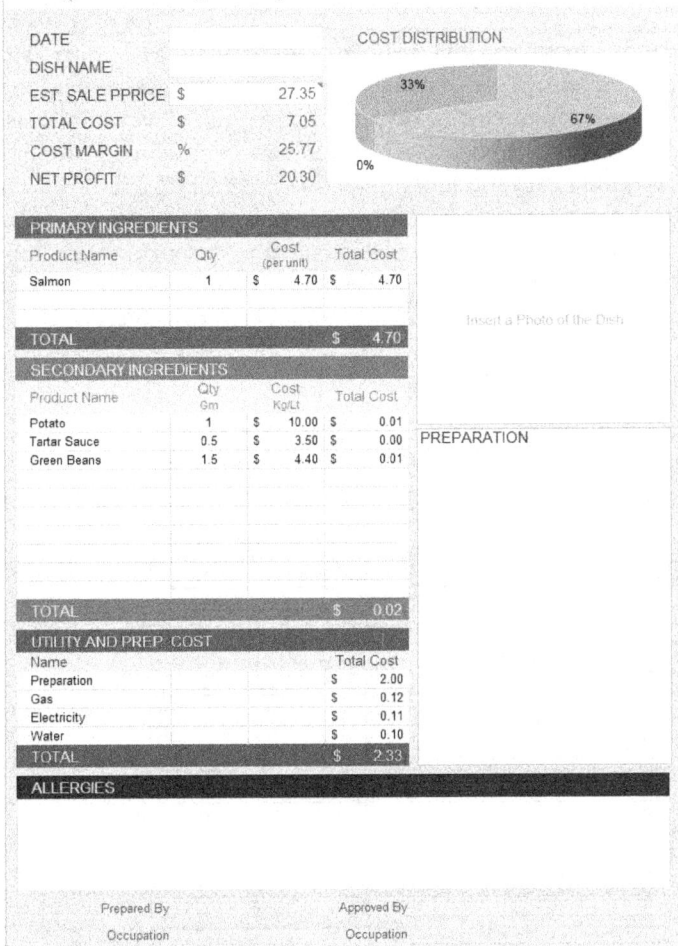

DATE		
DISH NAME		
EST. SALE PPRICE	$	27.35
TOTAL COST	$	7.05
COST MARGIN	%	25.77
NET PROFIT	$	20.30

COST DISTRIBUTION

33% · 67% · 0%

PRIMARY INGREDIENTS

Product Name	Qty	Cost (per unit)	Total Cost
Salmon	1	$ 4.70	$ 4.70

TOTAL			$ 4.70

SECONDARY INGREDIENTS

Product Name	Qty Gm	Cost Kg/Lt	Total Cost
Potato	1	$ 10.00	$ 0.01
Tartar Sauce	0.5	$ 3.50	$ 0.00
Green Beans	1.5	$ 4.40	$ 0.01

PREPARATION

TOTAL			$ 0.02

UTILITY AND PREP. COST

Name	Total Cost
Preparation	$ 2.00
Gas	$ 0.12
Electricity	$ 0.11
Water	$ 0.10
TOTAL	$ 2.33

ALLERGIES

Prepared By	Approved By
Occupation	Occupation

The tool helps you to price menu items based upon quantity, and portion size relative to cost. An example of its deliverable is depicted below. Email products@newbizplaybook.com for your own customizable copy of this tool

Beverage Costing and Variance

Among the most profitable items in most restaurants are beverages. Iced tea and sodas can be sold at a markup of more than 20 times actual cost. Beer, and wine, have lower margins, but are easily marked up, and liquor can be highly profitable. Tracking these costs and looking for losses through spillage, over pouring, or even theft by employees, is essential to sound business management. We have attached a screenshot of a tool to assist with beer variance below. Email products@newbizplaybook.com for an electronic version.

BEER VARIANCE

OPEN	FRONT	BACK	STORE	TOTAL
DOMESTIC				0
PREMIUM				0
IMPORTED				0
COOLERS				0

CLOSE	FRONT	BACK	STORE	TOTAL
DOMESTIC				0
PREMIUM				0
IMPORTED				0
COOLERS				0

TOTALS	PURCHASES	SOLD	USED	VARIANCE
DOMESTIC			0	0
PREMIUM			0	0
IMPORTED			0	0
COOLERS			0	0

MULTIPLE		VALUE		
GRID	SUM	DOMESTIC		$ -
0	0	PREMIUM		$ -
		IMPORTED		$ -
		COOLER		$ -
				$ -
			Ttl %	#DIV/0!
Barstaff				

One huge factor in insuring consistent food costs and product quality is detailed recipe specifications. Every item on the menu should have a detailed recipe with ingredients and procedures. The below is an example for illustration purposes:

Carrot Soup

Preparation time: 10 minutes	Cook time: 45 minutes	Serves: 6 to 8

Ingredients

- 4 tablespoons butter
- 2 medium onions, sliced
- 1 sprig thyme
- 2 1/2 pounds carrots, peeled and sliced (about 6 cups)
- Salt
- 6 cups chicken broth

Directions

In a heavy-bottomed pot, melt the butter. When it starts to foam, add the onions and thyme and cook over medium-low heat until tender, about 10 minutes. Add the carrots, season with salt and cook for 5 minutes. Pour in the broth, bring to a boil and then simmer until the carrots are tender, about 30 minutes. Season to taste with salt. For a smooth soup, use a blender and purée until smooth. Serves 6 to 8.

Variations

1. Garnish with crème fraîche seasoned with salt, pepper and chopped herbs.
2. Add 1/4 cup basmati rice with the carrots, use water instead of broth, add 1 cup plain yogurt just before puréeing and garnish with mint.
3. Cook a jalapeño pepper with the onions, add some cilantro before puréeing and garnish with chopped cilantro.

Chapter 6

Menu Considerations

A restaurant menu and its layout are the closest interaction your guests will have with the brand. Restaurant menu style, whether formal, or casual, should play off of your restaurant brand.

Your menu font and color scheme should match the guest's anticipated eating experience, both in terms of the type of food offered whether it be comfort food, or Italian South American fusion. If the restaurant theme is minimalist black and white with minor bursts of floral or artistic color, consider designing your menus to match that feel.

To save money, consider printing your menus locally, but do not skim on menu protectors. Unless your menu is very casually presented in a disposable paper form, expect it to be very roughly treated, spilled on, etc. Similarly, if your brand is high end, don't use a cheaply laminated paper menu with guests.

Borrow from themes that resonate with your food. An Italian restaurant may use color schemes or icons from traditional Italian imagery, which would be very different from those on a Vietnamese cuisine menu. Fonts, should also tie in here where possible

Descriptions should be vivid and enticing- enough to make a guest's mouth water. Food description is an art, and it makes sense to google menus with similar items to see how others have described them. Your menu, should distinctly reflect your brand, but what makes you desire a menu item will likely be interesting to your guests as well.

Always explain major ingredients (and minor ones in the case of highly allergic foods like peanuts, honey and shellfish). Also provide necessary warnings that may relate to hazards associated with consumption of certain foods (common for example with raw oysters or sushi). Spicy foods should be described as such, and your tone and word choice in laying out the items in a dish should match the style of the restaurant. If the restaurant is cheeky, its menu should be too.

Great restaurants brag in their menus about using organic, or locally grown/freshly procured menu items. House made salad dressings, sauces, or items such as bread can give your restaurant a unique feel that calls guests back time after time. Use these descriptions where they fit.

If food items or menu options or seasonal, or only available in limited quantities you can use those kinds of descriptions to create urgency in guests, and five them something to look forward to in terms of menu variety. Starbucks and their pumpkin latte, are a perfect example of this phenomenon.

Generally, the size of your restaurant should match your menu. Not only do widely different menu items with varied ingredients impact your food costs (especially in new experimental dishes), but they require space and labor for prep that will impact your bottom line. If you prepare tomatoes 7 different ways, an employee is going to have to do that prep every day, and the space it takes them to complete the task is space that is unavailable for other work.

We have attached a simple menu card designed for a small restaurant, but this something that a new restauranteur should research and spend time on. Local printers will be very helpful with fonts, layouts, and design.

Square Shaped Menu Card Template

COMPANY or EVENT LOGO

August 16, 2008

Appetizer

Heirloom Tomatoes Tower
with Organic Farms Goat Ricotta

Salad

Endive & Spring Vegetable Salad
with Fava Beans, Confit Cherry Tomatoes & Baby Asparagus

Entrée

Pan Roasted Alaskan Halibut
with Caramelized Corn & Wild Chanterelle Mushrooms
or
Grilled Prime Bone-In New York Steak
Peppercorn Sauce & Sautéed Fingerling Potatoes

Dessert

Chocolate Tres Leche Cake
Espresso-truffle Ice Cream, Kahlua Crème Chantilly

Chapter 7

Business Considerations, Planning, and Finance

While these considerations are often at the forefront of starting this type of business, we have intentionally placed them later in this book for a reason. By now, you should have a very clear image of the business you are trying to create. Now it is time to cover the business details.

Forming the Team

You may choose to be a sole proprietor business, but if you do that, you'll do everything on your own. If you decide to form a partnership, then you must pick the right partners. Poor decisions here will haunt you for the life of your business. Neither of these decisions has anything to do with the best structure for your business (i.e. LLC, Partnership, S Corporation etc.), which should be a discussion with your local corporate attorney.

Screening for the Right Partners

Choosing a business partner or partners, for that matter, is like choosing a partner in life. You'll want to be with the person in the long run, and if it doesn't work out, then you are in for a lot of paperwork. With this in mind, it's best that you have criteria when choosing the right partners.

One of the most important things to consider when you choose a partner would be track record. Is your potential partner good at handling money? Does he or she have a history of integrity or are there a string of problems or disputes? Do not start a business with others simply because of money, potential connections, or experience.

All of these are important, and can help you avoid common mistakes new business owners face, but you must be objective in selecting a partner, and if there is any hesitation, you should pass on inviting that person into your business. If that person is a friend or family, you must be even more careful, because you stand to lose more than the business if things don't work out.

Aside from integrity, experience, strengths, and record, another thing that your partner will need is a vision that is parallel to yours. What are the ultimate goals financially (i.e. we want to earn _____ in income), with respect to growth (i.e. we want 5 locations, or to use this venue to launch a franchise-able business), and what is the endgame (i.e. do we want to grow a business to sell it for a profit v.s. keeping it indefinitely as a primary source of income).

All of this should be agreed at the outset. As mentioned earlier, a business partnership is very similar to a marriage in a sense that if the partners do not have a common goal, then critical problems will arise. Find someone whom you have good chemistry and synergy with and whom you can share your business' vision.

On a final note, ownership percentages, and contributions of the parties to the business should be laid out and clearly understood from the start. Do not make the mistake of spending a ton of time or money, involving others, only to discover that you don't agree on these issues.

Each partner may have a different role. There will be partners who focus on investing money or assets, (these may or may not be interested in contributing time to the operations themselves), and there will be partners who focus on investing their expertise, (restaurant, cooking, or business experience for example.) When deciding on a partner, make sure that each offers at least one of these, and that their impact is reflected in their ownership. Keep in mind that equity must be very closely guarded, because once gone, it is very difficult to get back.

There are different of partners in a partnership with regard to contributions, but at least two kinds you should be aware of in setting up your business.

An active partner, also known as a managing partner, is the type of partner that actively participates in the management of the business. Managing partners could have also invested cash and assets into the business. Due to this, it is usually the active partners that have the biggest shares of ownership.

A silent partner is also sometimes known as a sleeping or passive partner and is a partner that does not participate in the management of the business. They simply contribute capital. Their ownership share is based on their capital contributions they make, since they don't manage the business itself.

A common challenge is that silent partners may have a nominal initial investment that gives them a material ownership share in the business. It is not uncommon for a restaurant to take off, earn well, and then resentment begins to build for those driving the business in being forced to share real profits with someone, who contributed an initial amount that seems small in comparison to the benefit they are realizing. This is why great care should be taken in giving up equity in the business for cash alone. If you don't absolutely need the money to get your business off the ground, it is better to avoid purely silent partners.

It also really pays to have partners who are in media. Whether you donate to a cause that will be celebrated by the media, or offer a strange food offering that is newsworthy, this kind of attention can make your brand explode. Many restaurants offer food challenges such as an 8 pound burrito that is free if it can be finished by two eaters in less than an hour. Not much exposure from a cost standpoint, but an interesting story, and often news outlets love these angles for human interest to mix into gaps in slow news days.

Drafting the Business Plan

After you and your partners have decided on what roles to play and how to split the ownership, the next thing to do is to draft the business plan. This is the stage where the big idea will begin to take shape. We'll go over some of the important points that you'll need for your business plan, and then we'll take a look at an example of an actual business plan, but first, why do you need one?

Business plans are required if you are seeking third party capital from banks, the small business administration, or other lenders.

Even if you are not required to put one together to get such financing, the initial preparation and planning is critical to the success of your business, and will likely help you avoid costly mistakes.

If partners are involved the business plan is even more important to insure the alignment of vision necessary to avoid later disputes that can threaten the survival of the business.

Certain items unique to the restaurant business should be included in your planning such as:

The Local Food Marketplace

The Market Analysis portion of the business plan is one of the hardest to make since it takes a lot of objective data gathered from research of both primary and secondary sources.

The following are some of the sources of industry trends data available to you for help with market analysis:

· National Restaurant Association

· State and Local Restaurant Associations

· Industry Groups (such as the International Foodservice Manufacturers Association)

· Hospitality Industry Databases (available at many colleges and universities that offer a hospitality program)

· Industry Publications

Some industry research and statistics may be called for here, but the best research will be familiarizing yourself with local brands. This means internet research of the kinds of food available in your area. This also is necessary to help with differentiation and branding.

Additional tools for help on local market information can be found in:

· The Census Bureau, U.S. Dept. of Commerce;

· State and local economic development agencies, such as Chambers of Commerce

· Small Business Development and SBA Resources;

The location you have already scouted will also come into play here with costs, traffic, and the other details described above. This information is also important to your business plan, and may come up in financing interviews.

Once you have worked through the local market, you will need to isolate the restaurants that are either in direct or indirect competition with the one you have conceived.

Direct Competition

This would be a substantially similar menu offering to the one you have in mind, and you would want to make sure that you are not setting yourself up to compete with an established brand in a narrow marketplace.

Look for:

- Proximity to your location
- Atmosphere
- Food quality and taste
- Portion size
- Hours
- Service and Dining experience
- Size/Number of Seats
- Franchise affiliation
- Food reviews

Indirect competition

This would be a business with some overlap in the menu, but sufficient difference in offerings that clients would conceivably be attracted to both businesses independently, were they to be at the same venue. Adjusting your own menu may be a way to reduce concerns that arise from direct and indirect competition.

Differentiation in brand and in product offering is critical to restaurant success, and should be a huge part of your business plan. This doesn't mean you shouldn't start a business that is similar to another in the area, but it does mean that you should do so only after working out how you plan to compete with any established businesses in the area. The strategy for success however is often more complicated than that.

Will you offer better quality food, a larger menu, longer service hours, or a better price? Perhaps some combination of these?

Business Approach

In planning business strategy, there are four basic business approaches that you can use in order to increase the likelihood of success for your business. These are cost leadership, differentiation, location, and hybrid.

Cost Leadership Strategy

This is very often the first strategy a new business seeks, and it can be a devastatingly bad one. Frankly, it should only be considered in a rare set of circumstances. Specifically this should only be considered for a very generic food offering in a high traffic environment. For example, if you are selling hot dogs, hamburgers, or fries in a non-descript location, and can move tremendous volume, reasonable profit is still possible.

To compete with this strategy, extra research is required to get the lowest possible food cost at a quality you can live with. Do not think that you will build a repeat following simply by being cheap. In fact, if not careful, you may send the message that your food is lower quality or less desirable in an effort to attract clients with low cost.

Differentiation Strategy

The next strategy, and one which much more often makes sense is differentiation. As the name implies, the differentiation strategy would position your restaurant in such a way that only you sell unique food products. Whether they are secret family recipes, hard to find food products, ethnic, or creative dishes, these products set you apart because they cannot be offered by others. Quality is critical in the differentiation strategy, but if the food is great, and hard to find, your brand can achieve margins which are much more generous, leading to higher profit with lower sales and effort. This not only impacts the overall value of your business, it means a higher return on investment across the board.

Location Strategy

This can be a very effective strategy, especially at the start of the business for insuring a solid, even loyal customer base. An example of this can be found with a provider we know in Los Angeles. He learned that a local clothing manufacturer had hundreds of employees, many of whom did not drive cars. He asked the owner of the company if he could serve breakfast and lunch to those employees, and remit a small percentage of profits to the company for the right to set up at the facility. The business took off, and now has a permanent location there, with constant predictable revenue to grow the business. If you are aware of an area that is underserved by local restaurants, or loaded with employees who cannot conveniently leave for lunch, this strategy can be very effective.

Hybrid Strategy

This strategy uses some combination of the above approaches to maximize success. This approach could combine both location and differentiation, while getting the extra benefit of spreading awareness of the brand. Others might have a different menu offerings at certain times of year such as Oktoberfest, or take advantage of particularly high traffic events such as sport, or concert attractions to take advantage of cost leverage strategy, while maintaining differentiation through a select offering of exclusive popular dishes.

Sample Business Plan Template

For those who are not familiar with making a business plan, here is a sample template that you can use for your food service business.

I. Executive Summary (This section would summarize what you are trying to achieve, a high level view of your brand, and how you plan to run the business. This would include an overview of what your business is all about)

II. Objectives (This section would state the primary and secondary objectives of your business. Here, you will explain what exactly you want to achieve for both the long term and the short term)

III. Mission and Vision (This part would state your business' mission and vision as well as the business values in order to show investors your approach – could include valuing freshness, sustainable foods, and or support for a local charity or cause near to the founders)

IV. Company Summary (This will discuss more on the information regarding the company. It would include the owners of the business, as well as their profit share, the startup expenses that are needed for the business, the location of the restaurant)

1. Ownership

2. Overhead Startup Expenses

3. Restaurant Location

V. Products and Services (This part of the business plan will go into a detailed outline of the menu that you will serve to your customers. You also need to give a detailed list of the ingredients that you will use to make the food that you are serving on your menu, with food costs and projected sales pricing.

    1.   Menu Description

    2.   Raw Materials Sourcing

    3.   Sales Literature

VI. Market Analysis Summary (The market analysis portion delves into studying and researching your market so that you will know how to make your moves to ride along the market and your targeted segment. This section was already explained above.)

    1.   Industry Analysis
    2.   Competition Analysis
    3.   Market Trends Analysis

VII. Business Strategy (The business strategy portion would aid in creating your actual strategy for the restaurant so that you will know how to determine your competitive edge, important relationships, how to position your brand in the market, how to price your products, how to sell them, and who to partner up with. This section has been explained above)

    1. Competitive Edge

    2. Brand Positioning

    3. Pricing Strategy

4.   Strategic Partnerships

VIII.   Marketing Strategy (The marketing strategy would cover the mediums which can be used to further promote the product. The two types of marketing that may be used are the traditional marketing mediums like TV or print and the digital marketing mediums which consist of social media and internet related mediums)

1.   Traditional Marketing Media

2.   Digital Marketing Medium

IX.   Management Summary (The management summary would give an overview as to who are working in the management. The organizational structure is used to showcase who is in charge of what and corporate structure. This section would also look into the type of personnel and job openings there are so that the management will know who may be hired for the job)

1.   Management Team

2.   Organizational Structure

3.   Personnel to Hire

X.   Financial Plan (This section will go into the figures of the business meaning the finance and the numbers. This section will first cover how to get the breakeven point of your business, when you are starting up. This consists of the expenses, as well as potential income that you may have for the year. This can be shown in the profit forecast along with the other expenses and the breakeven analysis)

1.   Break Even Analysis

2. Profit Forecast

- A note on getting financing: If your credit is bad to mediocre, expect to need a cosigner, large cash down payment (as a percentage of total cost), or be willing to put up viable collateral such as a home or car. Be sure you understand these risks. The better your credit, the lower the lender's expectations on down payments, cosigners and collateral. If possible seek out competing lenders to try to get the most favorable terms. A strong business plan can make a real difference in the answer you get from the bank.

Financing Your Restaurant

The clear reality is that getting full third party financing for a restaurant is nearly impossible for a first time restaurateur. Failure rates, high startup costs, and initial operating capital requirements are all working against you. That said, there are options.

Loans

There are essentially four loan options available.

Restaurant equipment loans are exactly as the name suggests, a vehicle for getting financing for ovens, and hard goods and inventory the restaurant will need. They are generally easier to get than a business loan, because they can be tied to the collateral financed. For example if the equipment loan is not paid, the lender can come get the oven. Though these are easier generally to obtain than business loans, they are not necessarily easy to get. Consider looking for specialty finance firms and/or leverage your great relationship with your local bank or credit union and high personal credit score to try to get these loans.

Business Loans

These are loans for the restaurant as a business. They can still be tied to collateral or inventory as in the case of an equipment or operating expense loan, but these are more generally available for the needs of the business. Third party finance companies that specialize in restaurant lending should be a better avenue for these loans. Have some experience, a respected established co-owner or a massively high powered business plan or this loan won't get off the ground.

SBA Loans

Surprisingly, more SBA loans have gone to restaurants than any other type of business. That said, they are still hard to get. You will be expected to give a personal guarantee, collateralize the loan, and may be expected to meet additional requirements for ownership composition, hiring practices etc. Take the personal guarantee obligations seriously. They could impact your credit for years to come.

Factoring

While not a traditional type of loan, factoring allows you to leverage inventory, equipment or predictable future cash flow to get up front dollars. This option is going to be a better fit for an established restaurant that is looking to expand its current location or open a new one. Careful here. A number of well-known brands have tried to grow too quickly, and regional market differences, or other problems have caused a successful business to be swamped because it couldn't meet the financing needs of a second, third, or fifth location.

To be well situated to qualify for any loan, you should be prepared to be tested on your business acumen, and financial planning.

Consider the following as you build out your business plan and loan applications:

Break Even and Profit forecasting

Crucial to any business plan are the breakeven analysis and profit forecasts. These two calculations will give an insight on the plan of operations, and your ability to repay the debt.

Let's take a look at how to compute for the breakeven points first.

BEP or breakeven point, in the context of a restaurant operation should be thought of in terms of:

P which symbolizes the price of each dish; (we have included a pricing tool, which we can send electronically upon request to products@newbizplaybook.com)

X which symbolizes the number of units per dish served;

V which symbolizes the variable cost per unit. Variable costs consists of costs that contribute directly to the forming of each unit of products (e.g. ingredients to make the food and labor used for prep and cooking). Variable costs are not standard and vary depending on the usage.

FC symbolizes the fixed costs that are incurred per month. Fixed costs are standard costs that you have to pay whether or not you make any money or not. Fixed costs are standard per month (e.g. electricity bill, phone bill, web server costs).

Now that we have the variables defined, let's talk about how to use them in a formula to solve for breakeven points.

First, you can look for the BEP in units so you know how much food you should sell to reach our breakeven point for the first year of operations. The BEP in units can be solved like this:

BEP X = FC/V-P

This is X (number of units to BEP) is equal to FC (fixed costs) divided by V (variable costs) minus P (unit price per dish).

Once you have the BEP number of units, you can now determine your BEP price. You simply multiply price per unit and the BEP number of units to get your BEP price.

It is formulated as follows:
BEP Price = X (BEP X)

Now, this formulation is just assuming that you have one product in your business. However, since you have a restaurant, you will most likely have a lot of dishes on your menu (including drinks and add-ons).

With this in mind, the more appropriate formulation to use would be to get the weighted averages for selling price and variable costs. After you get these two, you can plot them into your formula.

In order to get the weighted average, you can use this formula:
(Selling price of product 1 × Sales percentage of product 1) + (Selling price of product 2 × Sales percentage of product 2) + (Selling price of product 3 × Sales percentage of product 3) + (Selling price of product 4 × Sales percentage of product 4)........

In order to get the Sales percentage of product, you have to decide on a ranking of the products to determine which will sell the most to which would sell the least. The total percentage of all the products will equal 100%, so you have to split the 100% to all these products.

This is a place where the experimental approaches such as food trucks, catering, popups or small restaurant openings can provide real insight. If you use date from these approaches to inform your projections, they will have much more credibility with lenders and investors.

Once you've computed the weighted average of all your dishes, then you also compute for the weighted average for variable costs as shown below:

(Variable expenses of product 1 × Sales percentage of product 1) +

(Variable expenses of product 2 × Variable expenses of product 2) +

(Variable expenses of product 3 × Sales percentage of product 3) +

(Variable expenses of product 4 × Sales percentage of product 4)..........

After getting your weighted averages for variable costs and the selling prices, you can plot them into this formula:

BEP X = FC/ Weighted Average V - Weighted Average P

To better understand how to do this, we'll make use of a case scenario as an example.

Let's say you want to open up a burger business called Billy's Burger Stop wherein you will sell different kinds of burgers along some fries and drinks.

At the start of the business, Billy's wants to introduce 3 burgers, 1 kind of fries, and lemonade.

Billy's will be selling Angus Burgers at $8,
Veggie Burgers at $7,
and Bacon Burgers at $8.

Billy's would also be selling fries at $4
And lemonade at $2.

Variable expenses would include $3 for Angus Burger,
$2.5 for Veggie Burgers,
$3 for Bacon Burgers,
fries at $1.50
and lemonade at 50c.

Billy's decided that the Angus Burger will have an SPP (sales percentage of product) of 30%,

Veggie Burgers 20%,

Bacon Burgers 20%,

fries at 10%

and lemonade at 20%.

To compute for the breakeven point, first we compute for the weighted average of the selling price.

This would be (8x30%) + (7x20%) + (8x20%) + (4x10%) + (2x20%)= 5.6

After that, you get the weighted average of the variable cost which would be:
(3x30%) + (2.5x20%) + (3x20%) + (1.5x10%) + (0.5x20%)= 2.25

From there, we can plot the figures into the formula. Let's pack the FC at around $4,000 for everything including kitchen expenses, etc.

This will be 4,000/5.6-2.25 = 1045 units. This means that your restaurant would have to sell approximately 1,045 units to break even.

We have included a cash flow tool below. Email us for a customizable electronic version.

Cash Flow

When it comes to a restaurant's bottom line, nothing is more important to healthy growth than accurate cash flow information. This tells not only the financial health of the business, but will have a critical impact on food ordering, staffing, and other aspects of the business. A screenshot of our cash flow tool is attached below:

	Mon	Tue	Wed	Thu	Fri	Sat	Sun	Weekly Subtotal
Sales Forecast								
Sales	3,000	3,000	3,000	3,000	3,000			15,000
AR (Daily)	2,400	2,400	2,400	2,400	2,400	0	0	12,000
Opening Balance		600	1,200	1,800	2,400	(3,000)	(3,000)	0
Revenue								
Cash & Credit Card Sales	600	600	600	600	600	0	0	3,000
A/R Collected (<30 days)	0	0	0	0	0	0	0	0
A/R Collected (30-60 days)	0	0	0	0	0	0	0	0
Loan From Bank								0
Loan From Owner								0
Loan From Owner								0
Other Expenses Repaid								0
Commisary								0
Revenue Totals	600	600	600	600	600	0	0	3,000
Expenses								
Owner's Salary	0	0	0	0	0	0	0	0
Owner's Salary	0	0	0	0	0	0	0	0
Rent (Office)	0	0	0	0	0	0	0	0
Salary (Staff)								0
Phones	0	0	0	0	0	0	0	0
Advertising								0
Leads	0	0	0	0	0	0	0	0
Lease Payments	0	0	0	0	0	0	0	0
Contingency	0	0	0	0	0	0	0	0
Loan repayment	0							0
Commission	0	0	0	0	6,000	0	0	6,000
Synergy (Inventory)	0	0	0	0	0	0	0	0
Shipping	0	0	0	0	0	0	0	0
Contractor Expenses	0							0
Bad Debt & Returns	0	0	0	0	0	0	0	0
Expenses Subtotal	0	0	0	0	6,000	0	0	6,000
Monthly Net Cash In / (Out)	600	600	600	600	(5,400)	0	0	(3,000)
Closing Balance	600	1,200	1,800	2,400	(3,000)	(3,000)	(3,000)	

Start-up Expenses	
Web Site	1500
Furniture	2500
Miscellaneous	1000
Phone System	1000
Rent first/last	4000
Loan (JD)	
Inventory	10,000
Total	20000
Loan	75000
Starting Cash Flow	55000

Email products@newbizplaybook.com for your own customizable copy of this tool.

Creating the Profit Forecast

After you know how to compute for the Break Even Point, you can now go ahead and make your profit forecast. Your profit forecast is very important because it will help you determine what month you can reach breakeven and when you will start profiting. You will also see all of your expenses to know how to do some pencil pushing. Let's get started with the expenses.

Compiling All Expenses

Before you create the profit forecast, you must first list down all of your expenses. When you start your restaurant, you must think first about your overhead expenses which are the expenses that that you use to get the business going.

These would include the cost described earlier such as equipment, fixtures, buildout, inventory etc, the advertising, and the food inventory for the first six months.

Aside from that, you must already take into consideration the labor that you will use for your restaurant as described in the staff projection tool above.

We have included a Monthly Expense Forecasting Tool below:

Monthly Expense Forecasting Tool

	Month 1		
	Price	Quantity	Total Sales in Dollars
Unit Price	xxx	xxx	$ xxx
Less: Sales	xxx	xxx	xxx
Profit per Avg. Menu Item	xxx		xxx
Food Inventory			xxx
Rent/Building Maintenance			xxx
Equipment Purchase/Rent			xxx
Marketing Expenses			xxx
Business License and Registration			xxx
Utilities Expenses			xxx
Salaries Expenses			xxx
Bar Inventory			xxx
Miscellaneous Expense			xxx

Insurance			xxx
Total Expenses			XXX
Net Income/Loss			xxx

This forecasting table was designed to project costs on a per month basis.

It contains the price, the quantity, and total price in dollars. The price heading would determine the unit price, and the quantity heading would determine the estimated quantity that you can sell in the first month. The unit price multiplied by the estimated quantity will equal to total sales in dollars.

You will also have the unit price row heading along with cost of sales. In order to get the profit per piece, you have to subtract the cost of sales from the unit price. Under the total sales in dollars column heading, you will get the total gross profit for the month.

Right below that, is the list of expenses. The list of expenses are to be totaled in order to get the total expenses for the month. From there we subtract the total expenses to the total profit and we get the net income/net loss for the month. If the total profit exceeds total expenses, we have a net income, if it doesn't, then we have a net loss.

It is also through this table that you can determine how long it will take for you to reach your breakeven point. Take note that this tool doesn't assume any additional or prior capital infusion.

Determining Capital Requirement

By determining the income forecast, you now can determine the required capital infusion for the business. Most people are conservative and would infuse capital to cover the first three to six months of expenses whether or not the business reaches the breakeven point, counting on the sales to increase over time.

This creates a window to make mistakes, learn what real sales are, and what items on the menu are driving business. It certainly makes sense to revisit financial projections, breakeven, and profit/loss analysis every 30 days or so in the beginning to avoid purchasing food that you won't use, or incurring unnecessary expenses.

Complete the projection tool above, and plan for the number of months you will cover regardless of sales, and base your capital requirement on the number reached by computing the total expenses for a period of time plus the cost of sales for the said period of time.

If you are borrowing capital to start the business, consider negotiating a delay in the first payment on the note for 90-120 days to allow you to reinvest in the business, so there is sufficient capital in the business for operations.

Many operators are surprised to learn that well run restaurants or café's may make a profit of between 5 and 8% when all costs are considered. This is why food sales, and cost control are so important.

Chapter 8

Other Restaurant Considerations

Not all restaurants will have to plan for linens, or have a napkin laundry service for example.

Many will have servers, who need to know how to set the table to match a particular guest's order, other quick service style joints may have no such need.

All will need to deal with licenses, and legal requirements for operating the business.

Licenses

Tax – You will need an EIN or employer identification number. If you are operating as a sole proprietor this can be your social security number. Depending upon the state in which you operate, there may also be sales or franchise permits needed to make sure you are in compliance.

State Permits – Your state may have particular health or operations permits that are required to start your business. We highly recommend the SBA licenses and permits website for details. See **https://www.sba.gov/starting-business/business-licenses-permits/state-licenses-permits**

Local Permits – Your city may also have requirements for permits on health, signage, zoning, taxes, or alarms. We recommend the above referenced links, as well as the official city website for your town for specifics.

Incorporation

If you are operating as a sole proprietor, you can be personally liable for things like work related injuries, food poisoning, or the conduct of your employees. We recommend that you get counsel about the possibility of forming a corporation or LLC, which can help you intelligently protect personal assets from business exposure. Many states have the required formation forms on their secretary of state websites for free download.

Employer Requirements

Before you can hire employees, you will need to insure that they are eligible to legally work in your area. In the United States employers must complete I-9's which prove work eligibility, and W-4's which determine income tax withholding. For further information, the IRS publishes a tax guide for employers at **https://www.irs.gov/pub/irs-pdf/p15.pdf**

The SBA also has easy to understand information at **https://www.sba.gov/managing-business/running-business/managing-business-finances-accounting/10-steps-setting-payroll-system**

You may also be required as an employer to display certain posters for employees. This information can be found at: **http://webapps.dol.gov/elaws/posters.htm**

Insurance

You will want to consult a qualified insurance professional to discuss workers compensation, unemployment insurance, and auto/general liability coverages for your business.

Document Management

As your business grows, your need to keep and maintain documents will grow with it. We highly recommend having a fireproof lock box for key documents that do not have to be displayed on the truck itself.

You should take digital photos of all licenses and permits in case one is damaged, so you have proof of compliance while you get your replacement.

The following are additional tools we hope will be helpful in restaurant planning of various styles.

Food Inventory Template
(for full customizable version email
products@newbizplaybook.com)

Pack	Size	Unit	Desc	Unit Counted	Case $	Unit Price	Count	Extended
Dairy Products								
4	4.25LB	CS	Butter Chip Cntl 47 Ct Aa	cs	36.68	36.68	1	$36.68
36	1 LB	CS	Butter Solid Unslt Usda Aa	cs	67.09	67.09	2	$134.18
9	.5 GAL	CS	Buttermilk 1% Low Fat	cs	19.26	19.26	3	$57.78
				cs		0.00		$0.00
				cs		0.00		$0.00
				cs		0.00		$0.00
				cs		0.00		$0.00
				cs		0.00		$0.00
				cs		0.00		$0.00
				cs		0.00		$0.00
				cs		0.00		$0.00
				CS		0.00		$0.00
				CS		0.00		$0.00
				CS		0.00		$0.00
				CS		0.00		$0.00
				CS		0.00		$0.00
				CS		0.00		$0.00
				CS		0.00		$0.00
				CS		0.00		$0.00
				CS		0.00		$0.00
				CS		0.00		$0.00
				CS		0.00		$0.00
				CS		0.00		$0.00
				CS		0.00		$0.00
				CS		0.00		$0.00
Dairy Products Total								$228.64

Linen Planning Tool

TABLE SIZE	SEATS	54" Sq	80" Sq	90" Sq	72x120"	70x170"	90x132"	90x156"	96" Rnd	108" Rnd	120" Rnd	126" Rnd	132" Rnd
6'x30"	4	Overlay	16x29 Drop										
6'x30"	6-8			Overlay	24x21 Drop	Box	To Floor All Sides		Overlay, Pinned	Overlay, Pinned	Overlay, Pinned		
8'x30"	8-10			Overlay	12x21 Drop	Box		To Floor All Sides	Overlay, Pinned	Overlay, Pinned	Overlay, Pinned		
6'x18"	3 (One Side)				24x27 Drop	Box							
8'x18	4 (One Side)				12x27 Drop	Box							
30"x30"	4	12" Drop	25 Drop"	To Floor All Sides									

Linen Planning Tool

TABLE SIZE	SEATS	54" Sq	80" Sq	90" Sq	72x120"	70x170"	90x132"	90x156"	96" Rnd	108" Rnd	120" Rnd	126" Rnd	132" Rnd
30" Round	3	Overlay 12" Drop*							To Floor				
3' Round	4	Overlay 9" Drop	Overlay 22" Drop*						To Floor				
Café Tables	Standing	Overlay 9" Drop	Overlay 9" Drop	Overlay 27" Drop					Overlay 30" Drop		To Floor		
4' Round	6	Overlay Top	Overlay 16" Drop*	Overlay 21" Drop					Overlay 24" Drop	To Floor			
5' Round	8-10		Overlay 10" Drop*	Overlay 15" Drop					Overlay 18" Drop	Overlay 24" Drop	To Floor		
5.5' Round	9-10		Overlay 7" Drop*	Overlay 12" Drop					Overlay 15" Drop	Overlay 21" Drop	27" Drop	To Floor	
6' Round	10-12		Overlay Top	Overlay 9" Drop					Overlay 12" Drop	Overlay 18" Drop	Overlay 24" Drop	27" Drop	To Floor
72" Round											1 Cloth, Folded		
Serpentine	Buffet	3 Cloths with 2 Skirts			1 Cloth with 2 Skirts	1 Cloth							

Seating Planning Tool

Banquet Table

Table Size	Seating Capacity	Linen Size	Space Needed
6'	6-8	90" x 132"	11" x 7"
8'	8-10	90" x 156"	13' x 7'
Classroom 6'	4	70" x 170"	11' x 6'
Classroom 8'	6	70" x 170"	13' x 6'

Round Table

Cocktail Table

Table Size	Seating Capacity	Linen Size	Space Needed
2.5'	2-4	96" round	7' diameter
3'	4-5	96" round	8' diameter
4'	6-8	108" round	9' diameter
5'	8-10	120" round	10' diameter
6'	10-12	132" round	11' diameter

Table Size	Seating Capacity	Linen Size	Space Needed
2.5'	2-4	108" round	7' diameter
3'	4-5	120" round	8' diameter

Vendor Contact List Tool
(Have at least two options for key vendors)

Produce Supplier Contact Name _____

Phone _____ email _____

Address _____

City _____ Zip _____

Restaurant Supply Contact Name _____

Phone _____ email _____

City _____ Zip _____

Seafood Supplier Contact Name _____

Phone _____ email _____

Address _____

City _____ Zip _____

Pest Control Contact Name _____

Phone _____ email _____

City _____ Zip _____

Alcohol Distributor Contact Name _____

Phone _____ email _____

City _____ Zip _____

Repair and Maintenance Contact Name _____

Phone _____ email _____

City _____ Zip _____

Electronic versions of this spreadsheet are available upon request at products@newbizplaybook.com.

Invoice Template

Your invoice is as much a reflection of your brand as any business card. You want to handle business billing as professionally as your brand requires. We have included a template, and an electronic copy is available at **products@newbizplaybook.com**. Your invoice should include all of the following:

[Company Name]

[Company slogan]

INVOICE

[Street Address]
[City, ST ZIP Code]
Phone [Phone] | Fax [Fax]
[Email] | [Website]

INVOICE # [Invoice No.]
DATE [Date]

TO
[Name]
[Company Name]
[Street Address]
[City, ST ZIP Code]
Phone [Phone] | [Email]

FOR [Project or service description]
P.O. # [P.O. #]

Description	Amount

Total

Make all checks payable to [Company Name]
Payment is due within 30 days.
If you have any questions concerning this invoice, contact [Name] | [Phone] | [Email]

THANK YOU FOR YOUR BUSINESS!

Staffing and Planning Tool

You will need to have planned your assistance very well to make sure you are not spending too much on staff, and to insure that your guests are properly served. As your business grows, you will better be able to plan whether it makes sense to hire employees.

The following is a tool that will help you work through how much help you may need. We recommend adding 10% or 1 person, whichever is more, to your staffing recommendations.

Managers

In the beginning, the owner may be the only manager. Depending upon operating hours there should be at least one manager per shift (1.5 for restaurants that seat more than 100 – meaning a middle shift manager that comes in halfway through the lunch shift and leaves halfway through dinner to help at peak times). Large kitchens will require a kitchen manager both for food ordering, and training and management of cooking staff. Restaurants with large bar elements may also need a bar manager to handle ordering and bar supervision (the swing shift manager may take on these duties as well).

In fine dining or high end restaurants a Chef may be hired to bring exclusive menu items, or notoriety to the restaurant. This person would have kitchen manager training and food quality responsibilities, and in larger restaurants may employ a sous chef to insure that coverage is there for all open shifts.

Cooks

In the beginning or with small restaurants we recommend four cooks (on a budget the owner may have to jump in here when not managing). A day cook full time to handle morning prep and finish the day shift, a swing cook who stays through the day shift and helps get the night shift ready, and a night cook who handles cooking at dinner and cleanup/close duties. The extra cook should be used for heavy prep and/or peak times. Keep in mind if your restaurant is open 7 days a week, using three full time cooks per day, will mean 21 shifts of 8 hours each, so this may mean five actual employees.

Small Restaurants

You will need 2 folks for first 30 or so guests for service, food delivery and bussing. Add an additional runner/drink refiller for every 50 guests. More staff may be required if you have carving stations etc.

Fine Dining

You will need a server per every two 8-12 guest tables to help with clearing food and plates, and service of wine etc. You should also have a water/tea server to help with overflow for every four such tables.

Bartenders

We recommend a bartender for every 25 or so adult guests. If you have a more complex bar offering and a full service mixed drink menu, this may need to be adjusted accordingly.

Dishwashers/Bus Persons/Host Staff/Cleaning Personnel

Needs for these will vary widely depending upon the type of establishment. Cleaning personnel can be hired separately to come in at night, or responsibilities for cleaning can be shared among employees.

Bussing and Host needs will be greater in restaurants where there is heavy traffic and the need to ensure that no waiter is slammed with too many tables at one time, while balancing guest expectations on a wait.

Time Sheets

Many restaurants will have a computer system that staff use to ring up food that also has a timesheet component. Bootstrap startups might not. Below is an example of a time card template. Email products@newbizplaybook.com for your own customizable copy of this tool.

ACME FOOD TRUCK INC.

TIME CARD / PRODUCTION REPORT

WK END:

JOB NAME:

DESCRIPTION	MON		TUES		WED		THURS		FRI	
	LF/SHEETS	HRS	LF/SHEETS	HRS	LF/SHEETS	HRS	LF/SHEETS	HRS	LF/SHEETS	HRS
TOTAL / FT/SHEETS										
TOTAL HRS		0	0	0	0	0	0	0	0	0

Labor Tracking Tool

Labor costs should be closely monitored in the beginning to insure that these hidden costs don't overburden the restaurant. Below is a screenshot from our labor tracking tool. Email for an electronic version to products@newbizplaybook.com

#			LABOR						
1									
2			TOTAL HOURS BY:			TOTAL SALES BY			FOOD SALES
3	COOKS	WAGE	3 P.M.	8 P.M.	2 A.M	3 P.M.	7 P.M.	2 A.M	$0.00
4						$0.00	$0.00	$0.00	
5	KEVIN	$18.00							
6	DAN	$11.50							
7	ARTEM	$9.00							
8	PHIL	$9.00							
9	STEVE	$9.00							
10	SEAN	$10.00							
11	JEFF	$7.15				PERIODIC LABOUR %			KITCHEN LABOUR
12			$0.00	$0.00	$0.00	#DIV/0!	#DIV/0!	#DIV/0!	#DIV/0!
13	BUSSERS		TOTAL HOURS BY:						
14			3 P.M.	8 P.M.	2 A.M				
15	XINMING	$8.00							
16	ANDRE	$8.00							
17	WILL	$7.15							
18	JASON	$7.15							
19	DAN	$7.15							
20	JONATHEN	$7.15							
21	BEN	$7.15				PERIODIC LABOUR %			BUSSER LABOUR
22			$0.00	$0.00	$0.00	#DIV/0!	#DIV/0!	#DIV/0!	#DIV/0!
24	HOST		TOTAL HOURS BY:						
25			3 P.M.	8 P.M.	2 A.M				
26	JASMINE	$7.15							
27	STEPH	$7.15							
28	ANDREA	$7.15							
29	LAURA	$7.15				PERIODIC LABOUR %			HOST LABOUR
30			$0.00	$0.00	$0.00	#DIV/0!	#DIV/0!	#DIV/0!	#DIV/0!
32	SERVERS								
33			TOTAL HOURS BY:						
34			3 P.M.	8 P.M.	2 A.M				
35	AMY	$6.20							
36	JENNIE	$6.20							
37	CHERYL	$6.20							
38	CYNTHIA	$6.20							
39	CARLEY	$6.20							
40	KAREN	$6.20							
41	LAURA	$6.20							
42	MICHELLE	$6.20							
43	CATHERINE	$6.20							
44	ULANA	$6.20							
45	JESS	$6.20							
46	TARA	$6.20							
47	ANNE	$6.20							
48	AMY M	$6.20							
49	JULIA	$6.20							
50	ERIN	$6.20							
51	MELANIE	$6.20							
52	CHELSEA	$6.20				PERIODIC LABOUR %			SERVER LABOUR
53			$0.00	$0.00	$0.00	#DIV/0!	#DIV/0!	#DIV/0!	#DIV/0!
54									
55									

Sample Buffet Illustration Tool

Some restaurants will offer a home cooking, or buffet/steam table offering for customers. The below is an example of a potential configuration, that is also useful for catering business lunches or events. These can be easily drawn to fit the room and done with Microsoft Word. A detailed example is below, but you needn't be this specific.

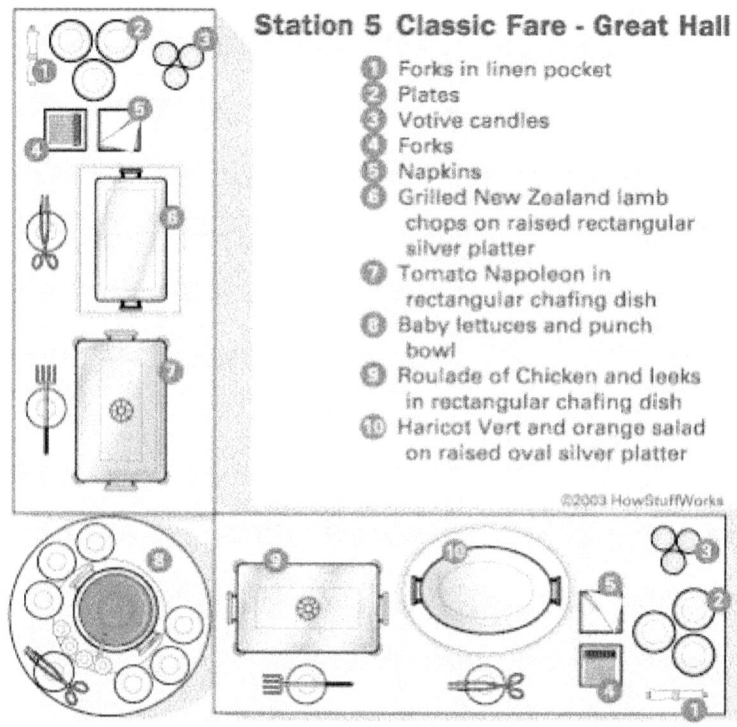

Station 5 Classic Fare - Great Hall

1 Forks in linen pocket
2 Plates
3 Votive candles
4 Forks
5 Napkins
6 Grilled New Zealand lamb
   chops on raised rectangular
   silver platter
7 Tomato Napoleon in
   rectangular chafing dish
8 Baby lettuces and punch
   bowl
9 Roulade of Chicken and leeks
   in rectangular chafing dish
10 Haricot Vert and orange salad
   on raised oval silver platter

©2003 HowStuffWorks

Proper Table Setting Design Configurations Tool

Not every restaurant will have the same level of formality, and it is totally appropriate for the owner to set standards as to table settings and configuration. That said, there are proper protocols for various table settings from which those standards should flow.

The following is designed to ensure that you offer your guests proper plates, flatware, and glassware in every combination. With multiple course meals in a formal setting, be sure to plan for extra plates and flatware, as this may be changed out during the dining experience. For purpose of these examples we have assumed water and tea for beverage service. Wine service is depicted below. This should be cumulative, i.e. if you are serving more than one of the below, be sure to add the relevant flatware. (we have included an example at the end)

Oyster or Cocktail configuration. (For Appetizer)

Salad Plating Configuration

Bread Service Configuration

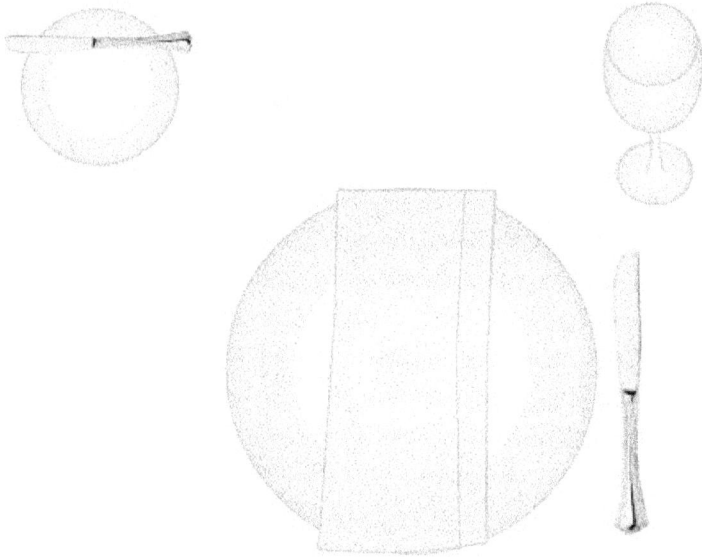

Soup Service Configuration

Fish/Meat Service Configuration

Desert Properly Served with Fork Configuration

Desert Properly Served with Spoon Configuration

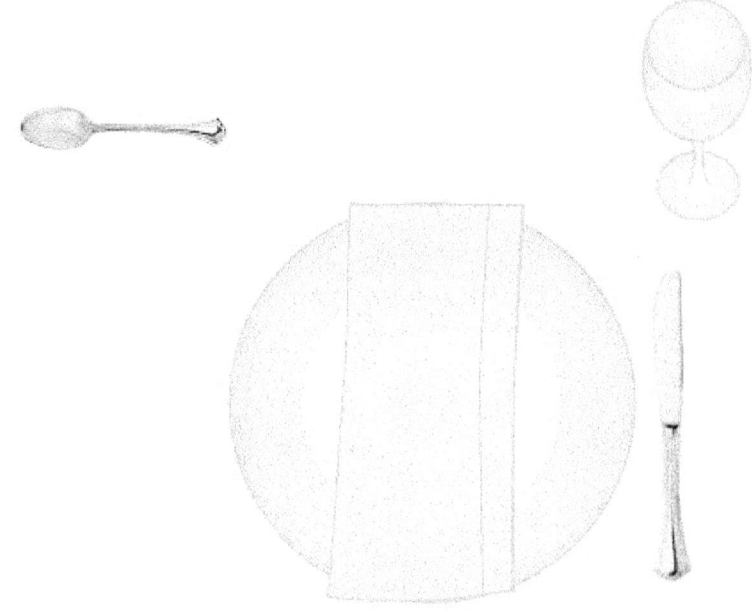

Red or White Wine Service Configuration (Note wine glass is positioned in the upper diagonal relative to the water or tea glass)

Coffee Service Configuration

Complete Meal (Shrimp Cocktail, Bread, Salad, Soup, Meat, Dessert {spoon} Red Wine)

Guest Survey

Many restaurants rely on secret shoppers, and guest surveys to ensure a quality product and experience for their guests. The below is an example of such a survey:

How Are We Doing?

We are committed to providing you with the best dining experience possible, so we welcome your comments. Please fill out this questionnaire and place it in the box in our lobby. Thank you.

Please rate the quality of the service you received from your host.

☐ 1   ☐ 2   ☐ 3   ☐ 4   ☐ 5

Disappointing   Exceptional

Please rate the quality of the service you received from your server.

☐ 1   ☐ 2   ☐ 3   ☐ 4   ☐ 5

Disappointing   Exceptional

Was your server...

Courteous?   ☐ Yes | ☐ No

Informative?   ☐ Yes | ☐ No

Prompt and efficient?   ☐ Yes | ☐ No

Please rate the quality of your entree.

☐ 1   ☐ 2   ☐ 3   ☐ 4   ☐ 5

Disappointing   Exceptional

Please rate the quality of your beverage.

☐ 1   ☐ 2   ☐ 3   ☐ 4   ☐ 5

Disappointing   Exceptional

Was our restaurant clean?

☐ 1   ☐ 2   ☐ 3   ☐ 4   ☐ 5

Disappointing   Exceptional

Please rate your overall dining experience.

☐ 1   ☐ 2   ☐ 3   ☐ 4   ☐ 5

Disappointing   Exceptional

How frequently do you visit our restaurant?

☐ 3-5 times per month   ☐ 1-2 times per month

☐ Once every 2 months   ☐ Other

Manuals

Your restaurant will need a number of manuals customized to your procedures, menu, staffing and operation's needs. Consider building the following in your library of manuals.

Employee code of conduct – what is expected of every employee of the company in terms of job description, appearance, behavior, and requirements of ongoing employment – may include disciplinary information as well

Food preparation – Addresses recipes, procedures, plating and food safety.

Operations – Addresses expectations of managers and procedures related to inventory, food and drink ordering, supervision of employees, and guest experience. May also contain trade secret recipes or other information not available to ordinary staff.

Bar Manual – May contain drink mix recipes (margarita mix for example), prep procedures, signature drink recipes garnish, and glassware, and protocols expected to be followed on intoxication and guest safety by bartenders and bar backs.

Training manuals – these should lay out tasks on a chronological schedule basis that clearly shows your expectations for both trainers and trainees. Below is an example for a new waiter trainee

Training Programme Week 1 (Waiter)				
DAY 1	DAY 2	DAY 3	DAY 4	DAY 5
Wednesday	Thursday	Friday	Saturday	Sunday
INDUCTION DAY	FOOD RUNNING	FOOD RUNNING	PASS	RECEPTION
10am – 5pm	3pm – Close	12pm – 10pm	10am – 6pm	12pm-8pm
Company Induction with Manager or In house Trainer	Complete test P1a (Pass rate 90%)	Complete test P1b (Pass rate 90%)	Complete test P1c (Pass rate 90%)	Complete test P1d (Pass rate 90%)
Core Handbook Issued – Ref day one checklist (Page 33)	Attend Staff Briefing	Verbal test – table numbers	Verbal test – position numbers	Attend Staff Briefing
Compendiums issued	Buddied with experienced member of staff	Attend Staff Briefing	Attend Staff Briefing	Buddied with Reception Manager/Full time reception
Waiter Training Manual issued	Ref. Training Manual Section 1	Buddied with experienced member of staff	Buddied with experienced member of staff	Complete Section 2 of Training manual
Food training Appetisers/Starters	Set up and Close down duties of pass	Ref. Training Manual Section 1	Complete Section 1 of Training Manual	IRC Reception standards
Health and Safety	Food Training – Pasta/Risotto/Salad	Food/Cleaning Audits	IRC Reception standards	Events (If applicable)
Complete a Food MOT with a Manager or In house Trainer	Table Numbers	Food Training – Pizza/Sandwiches/Desserts	Food Training – Mains/Grill	Guest Recognition Loyalty cards
			Epos Training	
			Coffee Training	

If you need an example of a particular type of manual, email us at products@newbizplaybook.com, and let us know how we can help.

Actual v.s. Budgeted Income Statement

These are critical for understanding not only if your restaurant is on pace to meet your and your investors' standards, also helps in the event you want to sell the business or seek further capital. Email for the tool.

Actual vs. Budgeted Income Statement
For the Period of:

	Actual	Budget	Variance-$
Sales			
Sales			$0.00
Other			$0.00
Total Sales	$0.00	$0.00	$0.00
Less Cost of Goods Sold			
Materials			$0.00
Labor			$0.00
Overhead			$0.00
Other			$0.00
Total Cost of Goods Sold	$0.00	$0.00	$0.00
Gross Profit	$0.00	$0.00	$0.00
Operating Expenses			
Salaries and wages			$0.00
Employee benefits			$0.00
Payroll taxes			$0.00
Rent			$0.00
Utilities			$0.00
Repairs and maintenance			$0.00
Insurance			$0.00
Travel			$0.00
Telephone			$0.00
Postage			$0.00
Office supplies			$0.00
Advertising/Marketing			$0.00
Professional fees			$0.00
Training and development			$0.00
Bank charges			$0.00
Depreciation			$0.00
Miscellaneous			$20.00
Other			$0.00
Total Operating Expenses	$0.00	$0.00	$0.00
Operating Income	$0.00	$0.00	$0.00
Interest income (expense)			$0.00
Other income (expense)			$0.00
Total Nonoperating Income (Expense)	$0.00	$0.00	$0.00
Income (Loss) Before Taxes	$0.00	$0.00	$0.00
Income Taxes			$0.00
Net Income (Loss)	$0.00	$0.00	$0.00

Posters and Signs

Electronic Printable PDF's Available on Request

NO Smoking
NO Drinking
NO Eating

In Food Preparation
or Food Handling Areas

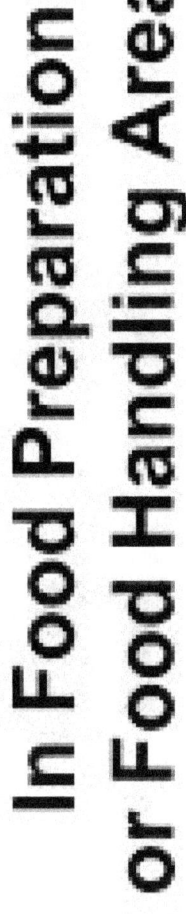

Food Temp

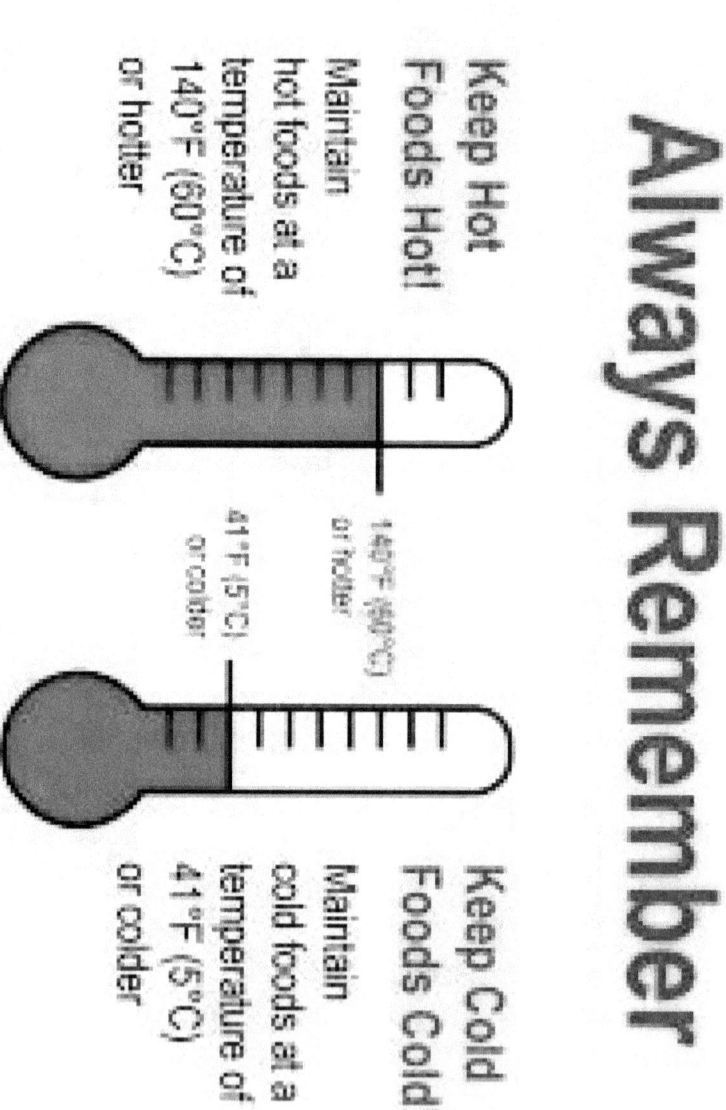

Always Remember

Keep Hot Foods Hot!

Maintain hot foods at a temperature of 140°F (60°C) or hotter

140°F (60°C) or hotter

41°F (5°C) or colder

Keep Cold Foods Cold!

Maintain cold foods at a temperature of 41°F (5°C) or colder

Employee Handwashing

1. Wet hands with hot, running water
2. Apply soap
3. Rub hands for at least 20 seconds
4. Clean under fingernails and between fingers
5. Rinse hands thoroughly under running water
6. Dry hands

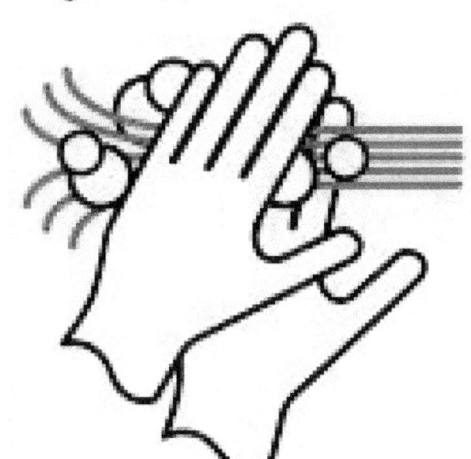

Lavado de manos

1. Mójese las manos con agua corriente caliente
2. Póngase jabón
3. Frótese las manos durante 20 segundos por lo menos
4. Lávese debajo de las uñas y entre los dedos
5. Enjuáguese las manos por completo con agua corriente
6. Séquese las manos

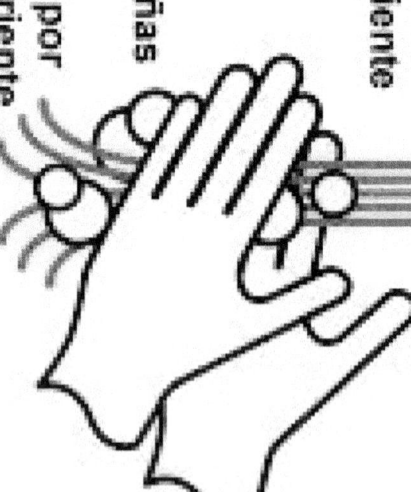

Virtually every jurisdiction in the United States has a requirement of a handwashing sign in the restroom. Check this for compliance with local requirements before posting.

Wash your hands

All employees must wash their hands thoroughly before beginning work and after using the restroom. Employees must use soap, warm water, and disposable towels to wash their hands.

Where?

Only use sinks designated for hand washing. Never wash hands in sinks where food is prepared or pots, pans, utensils, or equipment are washed.

When?

You should always wash your hands after:

- Using the restroom.
- Touching your face or hair, especially if you wear makeup or hair ointments.
- Using a handkerchief or tissue.
- Touching unclean equipment, work surfaces, soiled clothing, etc.
- Handling raw food, especially meat and poultry.
- Smoking eating and drinking.
- Clearing away dirty dishes, utensils, etc.
- When hands become visibly soiled.
- Handling money.
- Touching infected parts of the body.

Why?

Our customer's health is in your hands! Hands are probably the most common vehicle for the transmission of contamination to food and food contact surfaces. Good hand washing procedures are essential to the prevention of E-coli, hepatitis, salmonella, and staph.

Remember: cuts and open wounds must always be covered with clean bandages and the bandages should be covered with plastic gloves or finger cots.

Use of a common towel is prohibited.

Employee Exit Checklist Tool

While losing or terminating an employee is never pleasant, it is important to insure that critical items are handled in this otherwise stressful situation.

CHECK LIST FOR EXITING EMPLOYEES

Initial all applicable items:

_____Final paycheck, including final vacation pay-out

_____COBRA information for medical/dental/vision

_____Personal handbook/manual

_____Company owned software

_____Expense reports

_____Company credit cards

_____Laptop computer and any accessories

_____Home office equipment

_____Cell phone, if owned by company

_____Pager, if owned by company

_____ID badge

_____Keys to building, office, desk, file cabinets, etc.

_____Other:_____

_____Other:_____

The following items have not been returned:_____

_____,

but will be returned to the company no later than_____

Employee Name (Print)_____

Date_____

Reference Check Tool

You will be trusting your livelihood, and very valuable equipment, not to mention cash to employees. Check references!

REFERENCE CHECK FORM

APPLICANTS NAME:_____ DATE:_____

SOCIAL SECURITY
NUMBER:_____

POSITION APPLIED FOR:_____
_____

DO WE HAVE YOUR PERMISSION TO CONTACT YOUR PREVIOUS
EMPLOYER? YES_____ NO_____ IF NO PLEASE GIVE REASON/S
_____
_____

SIGNATURE_____DATE_____

PREVIOUS EMPLOYMENT:

NAME OF BUSINESS_____

YOUR POSITION _____

EMPLOYED FROM _____ TO _____

SALARY_____ELIGIBLE FOR REHIRE? YES_____
NO_____

ARE YOU PHYSICALLY ABLE TO PERFORM THE DUTIES ACCOMPANYING
THIS POSITION? YES_____ NO _____IF NO, PLEASE EXPLAIN_____
_____
_____

DAYS & HOURS YOU CAN WORK:

SUN_____M_____T_____W_____TH_____F_____S_____

PHONE NUMBER _____

INTERVIEWED BY_____

www.ingramcontent.com/pod-product-compliance
Lightning Source LLC
Chambersburg PA
CBHW071443180526
45170CB00001B/444